RELEASE THE FEAR AND FLY

L C Gillatt

Copyright © 2016 by L C Gillatt

All rights reserved. No part of this book may be reproduced by any mechanical, photographic, or electronic process, or in the form of a phonographic recording; nor may it be stored in a retrieval system, transmitted, or otherwise be copied for public or private use—other than for "fair use" as brief quotations embodied in articles and reviews—without the express written permission of the author except for use of brief quotations in a book review.

The author of this book does not dispense medical advice or prescribe the use of any technique as a form of treatment for physical, emotional, or medical problems without the advice of a physician, either directly or indirectly. The intent of the author is only to offer information of a general nature to help you in your quest to defeat and/or control your fear of flying. In the event you use any of the information in this book for yourself, the author and the publisher assume no responsibility for your actions.

Imagine for a moment the freedom you'll have once free of your phobia?

'It's all in your head!' How many times have you heard that? Perhaps you've thought it? Does it help? Probably not yet it's true, it is all in your head. The good news is - you have the ability to fix it, and with the guidance, exercises and tips in this book, you can free your mind from that fear to limitless travel.

Hello!

The fear of flying in this day and age of air travel is a nightmare. Whether its to go on holiday, business trips, visiting overseas friends and relatives; flying has become a way of life and affordable to very many people. As will become patently obvious – I'm not a 'writer', but hope you can forgive me knowing that I genuinely want to help you with your fears?

I have written this self-help book with my heart, and the knowledge acquired through my work with aerophobic (yes, you do have a special title) clients and after years of research. Minds can play terrible games sometimes, but it can also be a place of sanctuary – somewhere to hide when the going gets tough. The fear of flying though, limits you in so many ways, and in order to defeat your fear, old patterns of thinking must be replaced with new, relevant, healthy patterns. Just as you may seem to be full of fear with no escape, so it can also be full of confidence – think about that for a moment? This is not just a dream but a reality. Begin to trust yourself from this moment on, and through this book build on that trust. You can do it. I know you can.

Here in your hands, is probably the most comprehensive book on conquering the fear of flying. It gives you the help, guidance and information you need together with the tools, exercises and techniques to finally get rid of your fear and clear the way to constructing a new personal reality.

I've added links to people associated with the flying industry/aircrafts so that brick by brick you can demolish that wall of fear with confidence and knowledge. Be free to fly – there's a beautiful big exciting world out there waiting for you, seize this opportunity and go on an adventure of a lifetime. You do have it in you to succeed in this.

Yours with good intentions,
Linda C Gillatt

DEDICATION

I dedicate this book to my two awesome daughters Felicity and Nicky, and to my four amazing grand-daughters – Lily, Isla, Aurelia and Rosie.

To my friends, supporters, colleagues and clients for encouraging me to
write this book in the first place.

And not least – to the thousands of people who experience a fear of flying. Who courageously want to control their fear and get on-board – I salute you!

Index

- INTRODUCTION 1
  - Attachments explained 2
  - My Journey with a Fear of Flying 3
- HOW YOUR FEAR DEVELOPS 17
  - In the beginning – 21
  - Fear of flying and your children 22
  - Don't feed your fear – let it starve itself to death 26
  - Do media reports contribute to your fear? 27
- EXERCISES, TOOLS AND TECHNIQUES 33
  - Your fly diary 37
  - Neuro-Linguistic Programming 41
  - Watch your language! 46
  - Diaphragmatic Breathing 49
  - Method for Diaphragmatic Breathing: 50
  - Release 56
  - Hypnosis 57
  - Self-Hypnosis 58
  - Squash the negatives and turn them into positives 60

- Flick the Switch 63
- A simple 5 part exercise to deal with Anxiety Rushes 65
- 'Stop!' The Media 71
- EFT or Emotional Tapping Technique............ 72
- Roll Play.. 80
- Visualisation 81
- Get connected 85
- Mental Dialogue 86
- Modelling 88
- Triggers... 89
- Support Network.. 90
- Symbolic action... 90
- VAKOG.. 91
- Focus on your destination not your flight... 93
- Inflight relaxation, calming aid........................ 94
- My plane is a no smoke zone.......................... 94
- Change your fear to curiosity 94
- Other Fears and phobias 98

SUPPORTING AIDS 99
- Music to calm jangled nerves 99

- Nutrition 101
- Aromatherapy 105
- On-board Stretches and exercises 107
- Pamper not Punish 112
- Motion Sickness 114
- Stress Medication 115
- Flight Crew 117
- Laughter is a great 'aid' - seriously! 117
- Aircraft Tracking 121
- Comforter/good luck charm 121
- Worry beads 122
- Decongestants 123
- Apps 123

FLYING DURING PREGNANCY, WITH BABIES OR YOUNG CHILDREN 125

- Pregnancy 125
- Babies 125
- Medication 126
- Parental PR 128
- Child Safety Restraint System - CRS 128
- General information 129

ARE AIRLINE PRACTICAL COURSES USEFUL? 131
FLYING *IS* SAFE – SO ARE YOU. 137
THE AIRLINE INDUSTRY, YOU, YOUR COMFORT AND SAFETY. 143
- Security Checks 144
- Surveillance for Your Safety 145
- Police Forces 146
- Sniffer dogs 148
- Air Rage 149
- Alcohol and Flying.. 149
- Near misses 151
- Stacking 152
- Finally – when things may not go according to plan 154

FACTS ABOUT YOUR FLIGHT CREW 155
- Cockpit Crew 155
- Cabin Crew 158
- A Misconception of a Cabin crew's behaviour 160

PLANES AND THE FLYING INDUSTRY – facts, stats, and info 163
- Some facts: 167

- Facts about aircraft and how they're constructed.. 169
- How do planes lift, fly and land?................... 171
- Flying in general and your safety.................. 176
- Top concern from passengers who have a fear of flying is - Turbulence. 177
- Can doors be opened in flight? 181
- Can windows open during flight? 181
- What's the little hole in the bottom of the window?... 182
- Why do window blinds have to be up during take-off and landing?.. 182
- Why are lights in the cabin dimmed?........... 183
- Why can't I use my phone whilst in the air? 183
- Drones or UAVs 184
- Engine noise 185
- Flight Plans 185
- Flight delays 186
- Night flying navigation.................................... 188
- What happens when an Engine Malfunctions? 188
- Re manmade incidents:.................................... 189

- In summary: 189

I'VE NEVER BEEN ABLE TO GET ON A PLANE - *BEFORE* 191
- A case in point: 193

MONITORING, GUIDING AND GROUND TO AIR COMMUNICATION 199
- Air Traffic Control (ATC) 199
- RAF – Royal Air Force 201

PREPARE AND PLAN FOR A WORRY FREE TRIP 203
- Be prepared for delays. 208

A PERSONAL EXPERIENCE OF AN EMERGENCY LANDING 209

DOES WISHFUL THINKING WORK? 221

ACKNOWLEDGEMENTS 225

LINDA C GILLATT 227

INTRODUCTION

The first step to releasing your fear is to imagine that you can and *will* conquer it, then *believe* that you will……………………… This book will help you with that.

If you're reading this, you're probably in the 1 in 3 to 4 statistic of people who suffers from a fear of flying. Or maybe you know someone with this fear and want to help and support them to overcome it?

Aerophobics are people who break out into a sweat at the very thought of a plane. Who experience many sleepless nights of anxious anticipation before making a journey by air. And in not quite totally extreme cases – get off a plane before it's even shut its doors, to the extreme – not flying at all, rather, driving for long distances, going by boat or worst of all – staying at home and wishing you had the freedom to fly.

Aerophobics have many and varied reasons for their fears. In the years I've been treating/advising people, there has been one common denominator, and that is, their fear is *valid*. It has an original reason, usually long forgotten, and so sufferers think they must be…………'irrational'.

At the beginning of treatment, that's the one word I hear time and time again, "I know I'm being irrational." "I can't understand it. Am I being irrational?" And so on.

Let me state here, right now – a fear of flying is NOT irrational. All fears have a root cause, and with a fear of flying – the cause is usually something fairly insignificant originally, but to you, at that particular time – it laid down the foundation of future problems. Over time it has become overwhelming to the point that it makes you feel and behave as though you are powerless against a greater force. From that root cause, other negativities have attached to it, building, and growing until you find yourself dealing with a very real fear that…..well……because you see no real reason for it……..you put it down to being 'irrational'.

Attachments explained

As you progress through this book you will notice I make reference to 'attachments'. When something attracts your (particularly negative) attention, a 'train of thought' sets off in your mind triggering previous experiences/memories similar to the current one. You are not then just dealing with what's going on currently, but also all the previous memories which have *attached* to the train. In effect, you are not simply experiencing one issue but all that came prior that too. Think about this and notice how it happens/develops.

My Journey with a Fear of Flying

It's well past 2 o'clock in the morning on this chilly English night. I've just shut down my laptop after spending the past 2 hours helping, supporting, and encouraging people on a fear to fly forum.

Why?

- Because stats tell us that as many as 1 in 3 people suffer from one level or other with an anxiety about flying

- Because our lives are dictated to fast travel – for work, holidays, emigration, visiting family

- Because I'm a fully qualified Neuro-Linguistic Master Practitioner and Neuro-Hypnotherapist who treats people with flying phobias

- Because 36 years ago – I too suffered from a fear of flying

I was two years old when I took my first flight. It was from Rhodesia (as it was then, now Zimbabwe) to London. There was no night flying those days, and the journey took three days of flying in daylight, landing before dark, staying overnight in a hostel or hotel, then back to the airport at dawn ready for another day's flying. My memory of the plane is of a red carpet, lots of room, excitement – which by the middle of the second day was turning to boredom and, I suspect some difficulty in keeping me sufficiently entertained so as not to disturb other passengers.

As a family, we moved back to the UK several years later and lived in Scotland quite close to Prestwick Airport. Planes fascinated me so much that between leaving school and going up to Glasgow to attend a Business College, I got a summer job as Ground Hostess for Caledonian Airways. I loved working with like-minded people

INTRODUCTION

and looking after passengers arriving and departing this little but busy airport.

One way or another – flying became a feature in my life and I enjoyed it immensely.

So imagine my shock some years later when I discovered that flying had become a nightmare for me? That I never wanted to see a plane let alone get on one. That I anticipated flights with fear, insomnia, and trepidation to the point of almost being physically sick - I'm sure you can empathise?

I will never forget that extraordinary day. For me it was a routine flight. By this time I was an adult living with my husband in Melbourne, Australia. I was a model and catching planes to here, there, and everywhere was a necessary part of my life. This particular day I was flying to London on my annual trip to see my parents, one that I always looked forward to.

I'd gone through all the boarding procedures at Tullamarine Airport Melbourne, sat in the lounge with a cup of coffee waiting for my flight to be called, and thinking of my trip via a stopover in Singapore – a city I love for its vibrancy, safety and that beautiful old hotel Raffles where I knew I'd be well looked.

There was absolutely no warning of the nightmare I was about to enter.

My flight was called, I'd gathered up my belongings, joined the queue and sauntered down the tunnel towards the open doorway of the plane – as I had so very many times before. If I thought much about flying these days, it was more in the vein of it being incredibly boring. Of the seemingly endless miles and hours stretching out before me. Being fed copious amounts of relatively unexciting food, endless cups of coffee and frequent cigarettes to alleviate the boredom, because at that time there was no inflight entertainment except for magazines and books – yes, in those days planes had libraries, and yes – passengers were allowed to smoke on board.

As the queue moved closer to the entrance of the plane, my heart started to palpate shockingly. I broke out into a sweat all over my body. I felt hot, sick and very shaky. I thought I was having a heart attack or something really serious because it was racing so fast. Each step closer to that open door had my brain screaming to turn back. But who did that? No-one I knew. Then - I was next to step onto the plane being welcomed by a smiling Hostess. I tried to smile back but I was a bunch of shocking nerves and seized with a real need to get as far away from this plane as I possibly could. I also had to get on that plan because so much had been organised, and I couldn't back out at the very last minute like this. And as my mind was trying to talk some sense to myself, my knees started to buckle, I thought I was going to be sick, sweat from my forehead stung my eyes. I was bewildered, wondering what it was all about. People began grumbling behind me for holding them up. The smiling Hostess wasn't smiling any more. As I grappled with my breaking mind, my body turned and fled back up the tunnel, bumping through astonished passengers waiting to board, through the departure lounge and onto the concourse whereby one of the airline's employees stopped me and insisted I return to board the plane.

I never did catch that flight.

Aerophobia wasn't commonly recognised then, I didn't even know about it myself, certainly no-one spoke of it and for me, the whole nightmare shocked me rigid. As there weren't the same security restrictions in those days, I was allowed to leave the airport with the airline promising to send my luggage to me once the plane returned to Melbourne.

All the way home in the taxi, I kept thinking I must have gone mad. No way on earth did I or even – *could I* – understand why I suddenly couldn't get on that plane. There simply was no explanation; therefore a very real fear swamped me that I had had some mental breakdown or something. That fear gripped me so fiercely that my chest felt as though a tight band had been drawn around it, yet I felt a weird sense of relief that I was going back home – and away from that plane.

This episode was the start of a debilitating time of my life. I had no reason to fear flying so was left with the constant need to try to reason with it. Feelings of inadequacy and irrationality plagued me and set me on the road to relying on tranquilizers (as they were known then) to get through my daily life. The strain of having to hide this issue was stressful in itself. People didn't talk about 'mental problems' back then. And certainly, flying was still an exciting adventure for the relative few who could afford it. I didn't know what people would think of me if I said I had developed – out of nowhere – a dread of planes and flying. The few people I did admit my fear to would look amazed and say things like, "But it's all in your mind Linda, planes are safe these days." "Have you been in a crash, is that why you think you can't fly?" I'd shake my head and say no. And wished nothing had been said at all, that I'd kept quiet and hadn't voiced my inexplicable fear. These people said these things with kindness and concern but so many times I wanted to cry back, "I KNOW. I know it's all in my mind, but I don't know WHY? Help me with that, but please don't just leave it at 'it's all in your mind Linda'." The pain and confusion and shame from these conversations attached to this 'affliction' only added more to my overwhelming angst. No wonder I became a gibbering wreck. I used to despair that anyone would understand, that maybe someone somewhere would perhaps have a magic wand and go 'flick, flick' – you're cured.

Instead, I avoided anything to do with flying if I could possibly help it. I didn't even want to see planes in the air, or photos, or holiday brochures, or read postcards sent to me by friends. If I never saw a plane again in my life, it would be too soon. Because, each time I was faced with anything to do with the remote chance of flying – the whole confused, shaming mental conversation would start up in my mind and go round and around until I seriously thought I was going mad. It generated sleep problems, massive loss of self-confidence and feelings of isolation – as in – I was the only person in the world who illogically and suddenly couldn't get on a plane.

I was married to a man who, I discovered only a few years ago – suffered depression, so my home life wasn't exactly healthy having to deal with bouts of sudden verbal and physical abuse – again, something to hide because admission and seeking help was never an option.

He accepted an important position on the isolated Christmas Island in the middle of the

INTRODUCTION

Indian Ocean, and as I'd had to give up my modelling career anyway, I was in no position to object, and so – we moved to a place where the only way onto the island or off it...........was by plane. The Island's runway was so short only propeller planes could use it, and landing especially, was a total nightmare, even for ordinary passengers. So much so, that often the pilot would request we took the crash position and brace ourselves, and once the wheels touched the ground and we'd grind to a stop – the cabin would erupt into applause for the highly skilful pilot getting us there safely.

Life on the island with few residents meant a closeness whereby every moment of our lives was noticed, maybe not commented on, but there was a certain reliance on each other that you wouldn't find in much larger communities.

It did mean that when I had to get my prescription for tranquilizers renewed, I had to tell all to my Christmas Island doctor Laurie, a lovely young Australian man who was fairly newly qualified. He suggested that on my next trip to Melbourne I should go and see one of his colleagues who was using something called hypnosis in her treatments for clients with 'overwhelming problems' – no such thing as fears or phobias then.

In desperation to find anything to help me with this overwhelming fear, I did go and see her. With relief, I felt so much better after my appointment. This hypnosis seemed to work and thankfully I felt only a little 'jittery' catching the several planes across Australia to finally board my flight back to Christmas Island. Relief! I thought I'd finally conquered this debilitating situation.

Alas. Not quite. My sessions of hypnosis would work for a few flights but then tail off and I'd be back to panicking – not to the same original degree, but it was still there making me feel sick with worry and shame. I felt hopeless. What was wrong with me? I couldn't think of one single reason for this irrational fear. And I seemed to be the only person who had it.

Flying was still an exciting form of travel then. The world was opening up to anyone who wanted to visit other countries. I felt alone and unable to talk to anyone about it. What's worse was the added weeks of apprehension of an upcoming flight. By now I'd tried everything to get over the whole horrible situation. Tranquilizers, hypnosis, alcohol, smoking, calming music through my Walkman cassette player. I was crippled with the thought that I was, quite simply – mental.

Fast forward to nine years ago whilst studying Neuro-Linguistic Programming and Hypnotherapy with Michael Carroll of the NLP Academy in London. I was to be the class case study that day to 'collapse' a phobia. During the 'elicitation session' I mentioned I wasn't over-fond of flying. An understatement but I bet you've come out with similar descriptions because of the shame and guilt attached to admissions such as that?

Michael used several NLP techniques, including hypnosis to unravel my flying history – with all its subsequent attachments – and revealed a particularly vile session of abuse from my former husband immediately prior to a flight we were taking. His verbal abuse continued throughout the long flight, there was no escaping it so that by the time we arrived at our destination – I was a mess. I was feeling sick, sweaty, my heart racing, my throat raw from too many cigarettes – all the symptoms I had suddenly – and some months later – attached to 'flying'.

Once I realised that my fear of flying really had nothing to do with 'flying' per se, but instead this upsetting experience with my former husband – the fear vanished. And I do mean 'vanished'. Like a balloon popping. I revelled in this wonderful feeling of freedom and immense relief. How something that had become so complex could effectively be defeated by simple techniques was just amazing.

Since setting up my own practice in Cheltenham, England, I've treated aerophobics, I've spoken to people in the air industry, featured in GL Magazine 'Fright or Flight', researched flights, planes, airlines, and statistics and compiled it all to create this book to help you to release your fear and fly. This book is just the beginning of your journey. For it to be effective, it is important to spend the time – using the knowledge, tools and techniques here – to conquer your fear. *YOU* have to do it. And if you find it hard to concentrate or make excuses to not work on it, I suggest you use the Tapping Technique in the following Chapter to reveal why you have that reticence, clear it away sufficiently, then work through this book, practicing time and again, following the advice and *take control.*

Its important to think about this – the whole air travel industry is aware that a significant number of passengers have a fear, or certainly degrees of anxiety over flying. And so the whole industry works with that – on every level. YOU are important. So is your safety and sufficient pleasure to encourage you to fly more.

Throughout this book will be messages in this format (in bold and italics), please take a moment to ponder the message. Verbally repeat it, or write it down at least three times.

It is a message for your unconscious mind to absorb and assist you in collapsing your fear.

HOW YOUR FEAR DEVELOPS

Fears stem from so very many reasons. Some known, but most long forgotten or had never been particularly extreme to be remembered as the core reason in the first place.

Sometimes that initial experience held a shock as in fright. Sorrow because you had wanted to cry. Confusion in that you weren't mature or experienced enough to handle it. Fear and whatever emotion attached to that original experience must finally be seen for what the root cause was – and release it. Its like an anchor holding you at that age and time when you weren't able to progress or grow up from. Realising this, working through it with the exercises in this book, and releasing it may well have a significant effect on you. In other words, there may be tears, but they are healthy and therapeutic, cleaning out emotions like sorrow, regret, anger. Let them flow, its part of the healing process.

Most of my clients collapsed their anxiety through NLP/hypnosis/EFT and were happily free to fly. They knew that if, or whenever they needed a boost, they had the tools and techniques to quell any anxiety before it became a problem.

However, I've also worked with clients who had flown frequently before without any previous qualms, apparently waking up one day with the thought – "I can't get on that plane today."

Whatever the reason for their flight, a sudden aversion to it can set up all sorts of issues because flying hadn't been a problem before. It can be mind blowing. Hurried cancelled flights/plans, excuses given to employers, business clients, friends, family - making up reasons for not showing up to meetings/visits/holidays et cetera, because you can't possibly say, 'I woke up this morning and for some unknown reason – knew I couldn't get on that plane.' Which all sounds so weak and pathetic – even to you, and all the while grappling with a mind abuzz trying to make sense of this situation. One minute determined to overcome this aversion and get on the plane, the next – giving in to that little, annoying critical voice in your conscious mind talking you out of taking the flight and giving you all sorts of fantastic reasons to avoid it.

The choice is simple yet terrible at the same time. Contain the fear and make the trip which may very well turn out okay, but leave you with the 'experience' to deal with. Or 'give in' to this sudden fear and cancel the flight. And from the moment of making those excuses, all the other stuff comes into play to add to your original anxiety, overwhelming you completely. Usually first – justification for cancelling or making the flight comes into your thoughts – and I mean – personal justification not to anyone else, because *you* want to make the flight but...............

Justifications and reasons become part of your belief system which is strong and sometimes merciless. Not only will it not let you go, it will attract attachments, and so the whole mix of fear becomes toxic and all-consuming, and an exaggerated concentration is put on it, creating a trapped feeling of no escape. It seems that all around you are negative stories all about flying, and because of your heightened state of mind –

these become huge and feed your fear – you know what I mean.

It all seems so irrational. There. There's a word to make you feel helpless, controlled by a 'fear'. And if that's the word that you use to describe your fear/aversion – get rid of it – immediately!

Maybe now is the time to give you the meaning of 'irrational'? By showing you the meaning, hopefully you will see without doubt – your fear is NOT irrational therefore you can delete the word from your vocabulary and mind. Banish it.

Irrational: Not logical or reasonable.

Synonyms: Unreasonable, illogical, groundless, baseless, unfounded.

I think one of the worst words to use for your fear/anxiety is 'irrational' don't you? Your fear grew out of an incident or experience when you were unable to deal with it – it's that simple. Don't beat yourself up over it.

I am an intelligent human being, I am not irrational, my fear is not irrational.

In the beginning –

I would like to mention here, for the long term demolition of your fear, its necessary to get to where it all started and through process - collapse it completely. Some people still however, prefer to take calming drugs – and that's okay too providing they've been prescribed by a medical practitioner (please never take anything given to you from a non-medical person as they may provoke side-effects for you, adding to your anxiety). Just keep in mind though, that by using drugs, alcohol or other forms of a 'crutch' will only have a 'band aid' effect in that it will probably see you through a flight, but you will still have the underlying issue to deal with in the future. There are of course, a small number of people who find that taking calming drugs does get them over the hurdle of their fear and anticipation of a flight – so be it – whichever method – they've taken that flight and in time using this method to get on planes and fly may completely defeat the phobia – the repetition may combat and overcome the fear.

I should also mention here – your fear is unique, therefore your process to get rid of it is unique too. What is effective for one person, may not work for you, but don't give up. You may need a combination of aids – such as therapy plus a fear of flying course hosted by an airline. There are many such courses offered by airlines, and you may find it a good idea to go online and look for reviews of these courses before choosing the one for you.

Fear of flying and your children

Not long ago, I was talking to a couple of children who told me they didn't like planes or flying. Curious and quietly concerned I asked them why. One child told me they'd never fly because their parent had said they didn't like flying and apparently when the child queried this, they were told it was too dangerous. The other child began agreeing with their friend and I could see a copy pattern in this child. It's the kind of thing that happens with children at that impressionable age, or adults in a vulnerable frame of mind – maybe it's happened to you? With those children, I gently discussed planes and was relieved that their anxiety turned into curiosity, and I left it at that and turned to other topics to chat about. (It wasn't my place to discuss it further and I didn't want to overstep the mark.)

I know that the vast majority of parents reading this book would never wish their children the same nightmare they go through re flying. As a parent, you'd want to do everything possible to hide your fear. That's so commendable, but wouldn't it be better all round to overcome that fear and collectively all enjoy flights and overseas holidays? Perhaps look on this as an added incentive? It may not be you however who instils this fear in your child so please be aware of that? If your child has anything to say about flying, please take the time to ensure no seeds of doubt are planted, perhaps even discuss it?

Fear is contagious. The second of those two episodes developed as follows: my elder daughter when she was about 13 years old had a school friend over for the weekend. This school friend was all abuzz about her first and impending overseas holiday and she kept saying how frightened she was about flying/getting on a plane. The thing was, and I didn't think it too significant at the time, my younger daughter hung on to every word this girl said.

A few days later my younger daughter tried to tell me how this girl had affected her with saying she was frightened of flying. In typical British Bulldog fashion, I poo-pooed the very idea, pointing out to my daughter that she'd been flying since she was 11 weeks old (and by that, I mean a flight from London to Sydney Australia) and frequently since then with nothing to worry about. And with these fateful words 'Why let a girl who'd never flown before impress you with such silly thoughts?' and instead of destroying the seed before it took root – I didn't. I just let it languish in her confused mind to develop into a – fear of flying compounded with a future flight whilst suffering from tonsillitis.

If only I'd known then what I know now, I would have sat down with my daughter, listened to her perceived fears, discussed them informatively and rationally and never let that seed take root. I didn't. I believed at the time that ridiculing a fear of planes was effective. I was wrong – for many years too. Ironically she is now married to an Air Force pilot and flies frequently.

Let me give you this simple but realistic analogy – as a parent, there has to have been some time when another child has created an aversion to something in your own child despite your best intentions to bring up a well-adjusted human being? How about – your child enjoys eating vegetables. Another child visits, looks at the carrot sticks you put down in front of them for a healthy snack and immediately he/she makes a face and announces a dislike for carrot sticks. Now if your child is at an impressionable age, chances are – suddenly they too announce they don't like carrot sticks either. And apart from wishing you'd never let the visiting child into your home to create such havoc in the first place, what do you do to keep the peace? If you substitute those carrot sticks with something more pleasing to the visitor you are in fact rewarding it for its aversion – something your child will witness.

Two things come out of the 'fear is contagious' theory –

If you suffer from a fear of flying, please do everything in your power to not only overcome it for yourself, but also so that you don't infect anyone else with it.

Don't beat yourself up that in the past you perhaps passed your fear onto your child/children – rather make a point of discussing it with facts and information and respect that they have that concern. Although my grandchildren have no fear of flying, we often go onto the website Flight radar 24 where they pick planes to click on and see what airline they are, what type of plane, where they departed and where they're going to land. Its just a little exercise that's positive and informative and can be fun too.

Don't feed your fear – let it starve itself to death

Don't feed your fear, that's how it grows. Every time you pay attention to any negative story/report about flying or planes – you are feeding your fear. Think about that? Those negative stories/reports are nothing to do with you. They are not your personal experience so – why own them? Every time you pay attention and internalise them – you are letting them *own* you, and feeds your fear, the result being – it only gets bigger and more overwhelming. So what little thing can you do to stop paying attention to these stories/reports? Switch off from them, but please – go through your exercises to ensure that you've made no subliminal attachment.

Do media reports contribute to your fear?

Newspapers and television sell bad and sometimes, sensational news. The worst they can make it, let's face it, the more people are enticed to read/watch it. So to add to your fear are 'scary stories' splashed around along with pictures on front pages with horrifying headlines to grab your attention. You read it because you are already predisposed to anything going wrong with planes/flights ……………and in the process you add to the fear you already have. It's 'feeding the fear'.

This of course sets up a vicious cycle. You don't want to read, or in the case of visual media like television – watch the story, but just being made aware of an incident is enough to send an aerophobic into a mental panic, which in turn brings up any and probably all of what they've seen and/or experienced in the past, and all this is added to the current incident.

Can you see how your fear is fed? When it builds up this way for a surprising many of you, just the word 'plane' or 'flight' creates a very real mental and physical reaction.

Point of fact – in a UK free newspaper in 2016, there was the story about a passenger noticing a spanner had been left on the wing of a plane that was preparing to go down the runway. As if that story wasn't concerning enough to report, there was the 'what if' process added too, (It all ended well, the plane didn't take off until the spanner was removed). Yes, had it not been discovered there *may* have been negative consequences – 'may' being the operative word here. However, that wasn't enough of a story so they added another about a previous incident – which in itself wasn't really dangerous. (Incidentally, it's been an interesting process for this former aerophobic to read these articles in the interest of writing this book – to discover I can now read them with complete detachment. All things are possible after all.)

It's as well to notice how the media feed the fear – start to analyse why they do that and what reactions they want from readers/viewers. Break these things down into bite sized pieces of reasoning. Reduce them for what they are – sensationalism. Don't let them grow and attach to your fear.

Watch out for 'trick' words in these reports, notice how they're used to make the incident so much more dramatic. For example – 'It's believed....' 'A spokesman said......' and so on. Break them down to prove the sensationalistic way its being used. –

'It's believed.....' who believes? Why is 'it' believed? Can 'it' be believed? What does this add to the story? And why?

'A spokesman said.......' – who's the mysterious 'spokesman'? Okay, he/she's spoken but who is he/she? Is he/she a person of knowledge and authority? Why is there no identity to prove the validation of the statement? And ask yourself why there is no identification, after all, someone in authority or who knows the truth about the incident would surely add credence to the report? Instead the reader/viewer is provoked into entering a panic mode.

It's not just left there. How many times have you read or viewed a negative story about planes/flying/passengers and spoken about it? And given the source of the story? See how it works? The original story grips your attention, you read/view it and react to it, then what else do you do? Bottle it up or…….speak about it to someone else? Or point it out and relay where it was reported? See how it all perpetuates and grows into something far bigger than the original report? In a weird way – its good advertising for the media, and you're doing it for them free of charge and scaring yourself in the process. Not a good deal really, is it?

Scary stories like this are irresponsible but the media are in the business to make money otherwise they wouldn't survive, and the industry is highly competitive because there's so much choice for the reader/viewer to choose to buy into. Think about that?

A natural reaction phobics tend to have is to question themselves when faced with reports like these. They/you personalise by adding it to their/your library of attachments. Instead, begin to question the validity of these stories and work towards preventing them from affecting you. Or at the very least, make use of them. Read/watch them, breathe or tap them out of your system. Disarming them will arm you with power to demolish them.

The upside to this media coverage is that it makes airlines review and smarten up their safety functions because the spot light has been very firmly put on them and the public and governing bodies require immediate attention and their concerns alleviated by obvious action.

Knowledge is Power and I'm learning to trust my power.

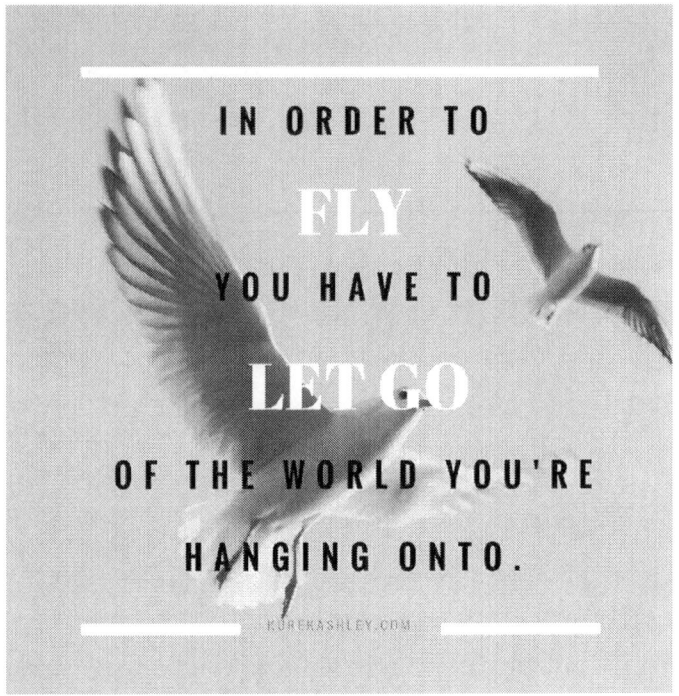

This is such a powerful message from my long-time mentor and motivator Kurek Ashley – the man who taught me to become a firewalker and to use that experience as a yardstick when facing tough situations. Kurek is an international Success Coach and author of #1 International Best Selling book – "How Would Love Respond?" For more information on Kurek and to watch his video blogs, please go to his website www.kurekashley.com.

EXERCISES, TOOLS AND TECHNIQUES

Treat these exercises as you would a training programme. After all, you are training your mind to change the pattern of your behaviour. The more you train the quicker you will be able to either defeat your fear or at least – control it. Start them as soon as you can to be comfortable and well-versed, please don't leave them to last minute.

Negative experiences = fears?

We've probably all had experiences throughout life that have created aversions or fears. For example, someone who's had food poisoning from eating a piece of contaminated seafood may develop a lifelong aversion to seafood. Whereas if you think of it – why should all seafood be classed in the same way as the contaminated item when it was only that piece that created the problem? Unless of course you have an allergy.

But what has happened is – not just an aversion to eating seafood again, but even the thought of it can bring up the experience of revulsion, emotions, and physical feelings of that time. (Apologies if I've invoked bad memories for anyone – it's just an analogy).

Our memories can be quite vivid, and when it comes to a negative experience, our whole body gets into the act. It's not just a thought then – it is a rerun of the original experience *plus* the attachments added to it – in all their particular glory.

Let me put it this way – you are given £100 (or $s). You open an interest savings account at the bank. One month later, you look at your bank statement and see the original £100 PLUS Interest on that initial deposit. The following month, you look at your bank statement and see the original £100, plus Interest earned on the first month's deposit, and the sum total of those two amounts has earned even more Interest. So each month, the money grows, adding Interest to the previous months deposits and interest until – at the end of the year, you have a handsome amount of money in your account that was generated from the original £100 deposit.

So your fear has *grown* and multiplied from the initial experience in such a gradual way that you are probably unaware of it until it becomes overwhelming and you simply can't deal with it anymore. Each time you are reminded of an unpleasant memory, the current issue attaches to the original – always growing. This is why some people experience real stress just trying to figure out how they apparently became fearful flyers. Its due to the invisible build up resulting in overwhelm, and as though that's not enough to distress you, there is further stress added due to 'where did that come from, I was kind of okay about flying before?'

Your fear therefore has a valid origin (no matter how insignificant it appears to your mind today), and armed with that knowledge you can see that you can in fact do something about collapsing it all.

It's so easy to think that because of the magnitude of your fear with all its other physiological attachments, such as feeling sick, shaky, sleep deprivation – which in itself wears you down, worry, stress to the point of completely unravelling into sometimes extreme anxiety, that your fear is bigger than you and therefore has control over you.

Lao Tzu the ancient Chinese Philosopher says it best –

"A journey of a thousand miles must begin with a single step."

I am ready to take steps to collapse my fear.

By buying this book, you have already taken a step. Reading it is another.....so you are on a roll – keep stepping until you reach your goal and you make that significant step in your journey – to enter a plane – willingly.

Do you begin to realise now that your fears are based on 'something'? That neither they nor you are – irrational? And by knowing that – you have more power to defeat it than you ever believed before. So take strength from that knowledge. And maybe take a few minutes to really think about this, to lock it firmly into your mind, to flip your previously negative thinking of being 'helpless' to one of being 'powerful', because knowledge *is* power.

Add these exercises to your new powerful thinking and you will realise the most astonishing results.

The thing is, you see or feel that fear as it is today, this moment, now. You may experience it as one entity too big to handle. That you may believe you are being – and here's that word again – *irrational*. Yet, all the time not realising that the deposits/attachments along the way have added to that original experience which, altogether has grown into a fear that manifests into making you believe you are out of control, powerless to a greater unknown force that prevents you from enjoying or making flights.

Now is the time to unravel it all. Bit by bit, step by step. It'll take your time, concentration, practice and patience – but your rewards are huge, in fact – they'll give you a world of freedom and enjoyment.

Your fly diary

Get yourself a diary or notebook specifically to record the progress, thoughts, and information of your recovery from your fears. This is important in that it becomes your 'fly bible' and you are making a physical exercise of writing, which in turn imprints more firmly in your mind – your progress, testament to your determination to defeat your fear/anxiety and ready reference to what works for *you.*

Date each entry. Write down these questions and answer with bullet points:

How you feel about flying now in this moment? – really describe it in detail and how you are feeling physiologically. For example, where in your body do you feel it? Does it have colours? Sounds? Write it all down, no detail is small enough to ignore, and this will become apparent as you progress and review your diarising.

Are there any attachments to it? Memories? Do they have sounds, tastes, smells, colours – Write it *all* down. Don't think any detail is too insignificant to document, because often it's those tiny details that give you most information.

When was the last time you flew? – Describe it in detail.

When was the time before that? – Describe it in detail. Keep going back until you can go no further.

If you haven't flown before but had the opportunities and didn't take them – go through this format, such as, when was the last time you thought about flying, but didn't take it? Describe it in detail. And the time before that?

Keep going back and further back in your history, reversing the process and writing down the details of each particular memory that comes to mind easily and significantly. Note how old you were (or think you were). Who else was with you at that particular time? What surrounded you?.. and so on for each entry/memory. This process is vital to defeat your fear and as much time and attention you can give it – please do, it'll be worth it.

Leave space after these entries so that you may add to them as things come to mind over the following days/weeks. Keep reviewing what you've written so that you may see the progress you are making.

By this due process, you will have a greater prospect of coming to the core reason, the root cause of your fear. See it for what it was and work on it.

How would you handle it/deal with it now? Be detailed in this, and when you feel you have solved the issue - collapse it, and allow yourself to let it go. Then retrace your steps back to the person you are today, but who now has the knowledge of what was behind that initial situation. And – knowledge is power.

Notate and document *everything.* Don't think anything is too insignificant to jot down.

Also in this diary or notebook, write a letter to yourself promising that you will stick to the exercises. This is your Personal Contract to strengthen your resolve and defeat your fear once and for all. Make this a real letter, an example of which may be -

Dear............,

I understand that this fear has prevented me from travelling – in the past. I freely admit that my thoughts have put restrictions on me that they are now no longer wanted. I make this Sacred Contract to myself to take control of my fear and defeat it completely. I will undergo the process I must make with courage and determination. To faithfully practice these exercises which I know will help me with my mission. And I acknowledge and respect my reasons for having developed my fear in the first place. I promise to release it completely with honour and love. I understand it no longer serves a purpose.

Signed......................... and date it.

Bookmark the page in your diary so that any time you feel the stirrings of the anxiety, you can reread it and reaffirm your determination to beat it. And yes, some of you may find this letter a bit 'weird' but bear with me?

> *I am prepared to open my mind to new opportunities to release me of my fears.*

Neuro-Linguistic Programming

NLP is a programme of communication, personal development, change of behaviour patterns, and associated psychotherapy created by Dr John Grinder and Richard Bandler in California in the 1970s. It works on the three basic tenets of our minds, those being - neurology, language and programming.

To quote my teacher and facilitator Michael Carroll of the NLP Academy near London –

> *"Understanding your Mind; Conscious and Unconscious Processing*

How to utilise the recourses of your unconscious mind

In this article, I will present a much-used metaphor in NLP and that is the notion of a conscious and unconscious mind. I use the word metaphor because neither the conscious or unconscious mind exists in the literal sense. The terms are just useful to package conscious and unconscious processing.

Clients come to see me because they want to change something in their life. What they are really seeking is to change the way they create their maps of the world; they never quite say it like that though. The clients are living in a story. Now while they are the central character in that story, they have problems because they are creating the story unconsciously. In most cases clients use their conscious mind to wrestle control of the problems without explicitly including the unconscious mind in the change. This is an error and one that New Code NLP seeks to correct. When we engage the unconscious mind, the change will be lasting. It's all a matter of good communication between the conscious and unconscious mind."

http://www.nlpacademy.co.uk/articles/view/understanding_your_mind_conscious_and_unconscious_processing/

I recommend the NLP Academy as being in the forefront of 'change management'.
More information re NLP, plus videos - www.nlpacademy.co.uk

I also recommend that should you wish to personally attend an NLP Therapist and/or hypnotherapist for your fear, check to see if there is an NLP Academy trained person near you by posting a request on their Facebook Page – NLP Academy https://www.facebook.com/NLP-Academy-155371461150012/?fref=ts and who knows, maybe like me, you may wish to become a qualified NLP Practitioner and/or Hypnotherapist. The NLP Academy has very close associations with Founder Dr John Grinder and other highly respected teachers, and I recommend them highly.

I explain to my clients that their unconscious mind is like a personal 'computer'. It has within itself – all your experiences, learned behaviour, all the information you've taken in from birth to now. It can analyse it all and create solutions because it makes intuitive judgements.

When faced with a decision, the 'chatter' in our conscious mind starts up and blurs information as to which is the better decision to take, and sometimes talks you out of making the decision completely. Whereas, your unconscious mind extracts all relevant information pertaining to making the 'right' decision (for you) and is ready to give it to you. Invariably though, the 'chatter' over-rules.

However, if that is not the 'right' decision to make, your unconscious mind gives you a physiological nudge, saying, "Hey, I've got the right decision for you. Pay attention to me." And where do you experience that physiological nudge? If I said, 'gut feeling' – do you have a eureka moment and begin to understand how powerful that part of your brain is?

And, which usually turns out to be the 'right' decision for you? The chatter or the gut?

Diagram depicting Conscious and Unconscious minds:

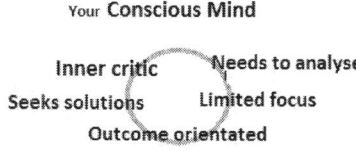

Your **Conscious Mind**

Inner critic   Needs to analyse
Seeks solutions   Limited focus
Outcome orientated

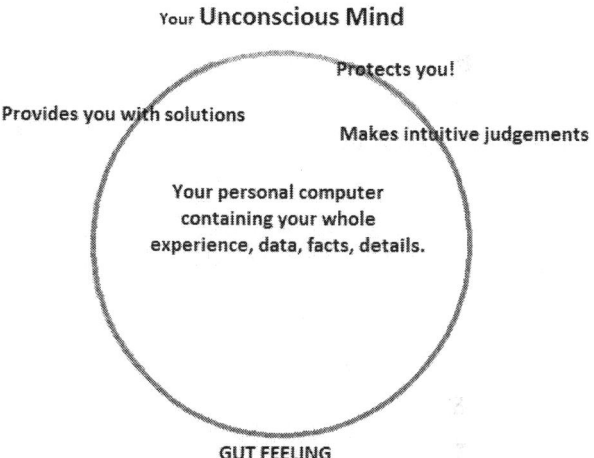

Your **Unconscious Mind**

Protects you!
Provides you with solutions
Makes intuitive judgements

Your personal computer containing your whole experience, data, facts, details.

GUT FEELING

Pronounced scale of both predominant sections of your mind to underline the importance and function of each.

I must learn to trust my gut feeling its helped me in the past.

Watch your language!

You've probably heard the saying, "Sticks and stones can break my bones, but words can never harm me." Experience tells us that in actual fact – words can break you – harsh, negative words can certainly break you. It's 'who' is saying the words that can really undo you. If it's another person, you have a choice. You can rebut them, ignore them, or keep silent but mentally clobber them.

But what do you do when your harshest critic is...........yourself? You know what I mean, that little voice that demolishes your positive intentions, plans, ideas, before they become actions. The one that says, 'You kidding? You really think you should do that? Isn't it better to live with what you know without changing things? You think you're good enough for that?' And so, you listen to that voice and with a heave of regret – do/say nothing and revert back to 'normal'. But does that silence your inner critic? No, your mental conversation then clings to, 'why don't I...........' And so your mind goes onto a never ending loop of negativity.

So what can you do about this? Firstly, begin to change your actual language. Instead of saying, 'I can't because...........' change that to a qualifier. For example, 'I can't right now, but right now, I will work on changing that.' This may seem clumsy but view it as a process.

As someone who works with clients to defeat their fear of flying, I use a combination of NLP, Hypnosis and EFT (Tapping) as well as Diaphragmatic Breathing. Clients who have been unable to attend me in person have found, that by using my techniques and spending time practicing the exercises over and over again – they do manage to either get over their fears completely or at least 'manage' them.

They begin to realise they have the power at their fingertips to help them through the whole process of flying – so it IS possible – you just have to put in the time and effort, and at the end of the day, your feelings of self-satisfaction in defeating something that held you in such fear will fill you with courage, happiness and a new sense of freedom that will quite likely spread through your life.

Please follow my sequence of exercises because they are a natural progression to help you overcome your fear or at the very least – to understand it, and usually if you understand why you were nervous, you have a better chance of dealing with it or overcoming it. Its when you are grappling with the 'unknown' or repression that problems arise because the dilemma creates a loop which goes round and around your mind with no solution but to frustrate and weaken any resolve, and often adds to your stress levels and anxiety.

I suggest also, that you have a particular piece of music playing in the background whilst going through your exercises. Subliminally this music will attach to your exercises until there comes a time when, just hearing that piece of music will automatically sooth you. The choice of music is entirely up to you, I do however recommend that it is new so there are no attachments to it, and that It is purely music with no lyrics. Ambient music is particularly recommended, and to help you, I have given you details of two composers of calming music in the Chapter Supporting Aids page.

Diaphragmatic Breathing

If you watch a newborn or very young baby sleeping, you will invariably see both its chest and stomach moving up and down – up on the inhale, down on the exhale.

This was our original and natural form of breathing which gave us calm and peace. Unfortunately with the stressful lives we lead to today, our form of usual breathing is shallow and quick. This sets up a whole lot of disadvantages. (Small exercise here, check your breathing right now. Is it shallow or deep?)

Diaphragmatic breathing as a normal form of breathing will generally lower stress, maintain focus, control, and calmness because it is drawing more oxygen into your system allowing for good mental processing for clearer judgment; instantly lifts energy levels, and increases feelings of control. As well as freeing your system and blood supply from stress hormones, it promotes more lovely endorphins and releases natural chemicals like Oxytocin, Prolactin into your system too, creating overall feelings of wellbeing. (Endorphins – your body's naturally created 'morphine' dulls pain and sets off big doses of euphoria, or 'feel good feelings'.)

Faced with a potentially anxious experience – ie 'flying' – breathing fully will allow you to feel more in control, focused and positive. Please don't discard the fact that although this is a very simple exercise – it is incredibly powerful.

This method of breathing is also the introduction to hypnosis, or in your case – if you practice sufficiently – will put you into a deep relaxed state akin to self-hypnosis, which will help you to control pre-flight nerves.

I highly advise you do this exercise with your background music to add to the feelings of well-being, calm and peace.

Method for Diaphragmatic Breathing:

Either sit or lie comfortably with your neck and head supported, turn off your phone and ensure that you won't be disturbed – certainly whilst you are practicing your breathing.

Position your hands so that your thumbs rest just below the bottom ribs on either side of your ribcage. Link your fingers together. Watch your hands as you begin to breathe deeply. This is an initial yet visual demonstration to show you how deeply you should breathe, once you've got the knack of diaphragmatic breathing you'll no longer have to place your hands like this and instead take up a more comfortable position.

As you breathe in – watch your hands rise, pushing upwards as far as they will go as your lungs fill with air.

As you breathe out – watch your hands fall comfortably back into the original position.

After taking a few of these breaths, whisper the word 'release' or 'relax' under your breath using the length of your exhale, as in R-e-e-e-e-l-l-l-a-a-a-a-a-x.

Next, introduce an imaginary wave of calm, starting from the top of your head. Slowly, and bit by bit, let that wave flow through your each of your muscles in your entire body right down to your toes.

Each time you inhale, draw this wave of relaxation through your body piece by piece.

With your exhale, spread that wave out and feel it spreading – it's a lovely feeling btw.

Pay particular attention to the areas of your body that feel especially 'tight' and spend some little time breathing calm into those areas. 'Relax' and 'Release' any tightness, then move onto the next area.

Sequence for Diaphragmatic Breathing, start from your head and work down your body.

- Head
- Face – forehead, ears, around your eyes, cheeks, jaw
- Back of the head down to your nape
- Around your shoulder blades
- Down your arms, through your hands and down your fingers to the tips
- Chest
- Spine – vertebrae by vertebrae
- Stomach
- Pelvis

- Posterior
- Hips
- Thighs
- Calves
- Ankles
- Feet
- Toes

Once you have taken this wave of relaxation through your body from the very top of your head to your toes, start the process again, scanning your body for any remaining tension, relax and release that area and continue.

Allow your breathing to return to your normal state.

Its preferable to breathe in through your nose and out through your mouth, but it's the deep breathing that's important so whichever way you do it – is good.

After scanning your body, you may find counting up to 5 as you breathe in, pause for a count of 3 then release your breath slowly will help because your attention is focused on counting rather than the 'chatter' in your conscious mind. I find its more important to find *your* way to do this exercise because you are more likely to maintain it until it becomes second nature. Never hold your breath though because that can be counterproductive.

More explanation of the benefits of diaphragmatically breathing will be found in my '5 Simple Steps To Stop Panic Attacks' – although I prefer to call them 'Anxiety Rushes' because 'panic' can be perceived as being counter-productive. Notice the difference in the effect they have on you. The change in language takes the 'drama' out of 'panic' and 'attack'. – Think about it and try it out a few times. How surprised will you be to notice that difference?

Training yourself to breathe like this may take only a couple of days, or a couple of weeks so please don't despair if its not instant, after all you've spent most of your life shallow breathing so it figures that it may take time to turn this into your natural way of breathing.

Create a rhythm of breathing, counting and scanning. At some stage you may want to replace the 'counting' with a mantra. Something simple like – 'I am strong.', 'I am determined.', 'I can do this.' and so on.

Let it be a simple mantra and just repeat it over and over again. You can further reinforce your mantra with the action of pressing your thumb and pointing finger together and saying "I", pressing your thumb and next finger and saying "can", thumb pressing your ring finger "do", thumb pressing your pinkie finger "this." – This is a particularly good exercise for people who need to *feel* in control because their dominant sense is kinaesthetic, they are more tactile.

Tactile mantras are a really good exercise because you can do them without feeling foolish if other people are around.

You will find the combination of diaphragmatic breathing and repeating your mantra will help to calm you under most circumstances and areas of your life, so it is worth the effort to make it your normal form of breathing.

Don't leave these aids too late though because that would be asking too much of them and you. As soon as you feel a 'flutter' in your chest or stomach – dive into them immediately.

Gradually introduce your deep breathing into other areas of your life. Do leave out the scanning though whilst driving a car, on a motor bike or if you are working with machinery – areas that you need to be fully aware and conscious.

Note: Remember - improper breathing leads to tension, stress, anxiety, ill health.

Whenever you sit at a stoplight, are waiting in a queue, or watching television, take a diaphragmatic breath. Whenever you sit down to read a book or lie down to rest, start with a tummy breath. Whenever you think about your body, your health, take a diaphragmatic breath. Practice starts now. Happy Breathing.

Release.......

A useful trick as mentioned before in this chapter – as you exhale, stretch the word 'release' or 'relax' under your breath for as long as the breath takes. This can be used immediately and I use a sequence of diaphragmatic breaths with my clients to prepare them for hypnosis. You will be able to use it for self-hypnosis which will induce feelings of calm and control. Every time your mind starts to wander, bring it back to focusing on your breathing. This technique takes some practice but the rewards are worth your time and effort.

Hypnosis

If you are a novice to hypnosis you may initially be reticent to try it because your thoughts may be created from stage shows of people acting like manic chickens, eating onions as apples and generally doing all the things you'd stay well away from.

Hypnosis is really nothing like that. What if I were to tell you that you will NEVER do or say anything under hypnosis that would go against your own moral code and judgement? Its true, so you may think what you like about those manic people chickens.

Self-Hypnosis

It may surprise you to learn that there would were occasions in your life when you experienced a form of self-hypnosis. Those times when the 'chatter' in your mind had been replaced with what seems like a peaceful 'silence'?

I give this analogy to my clients –

Imagine a time that you are faced with a long car journey as the driver. You've had a good night's sleep and completely awake and alert. You get on the motorway or freeway at Junction 7. Your exit road from the motorway/freeway is Junction 32. So you settle into your long drive. Maybe you have the radio on. If you're travelling with companions, conversation may dwindle as the journey progresses. Initially you notice the numbers of the junctions as you pass them – 9, 10, 11 – and so on. Until suddenly you see a sign saying Junction 28 and you wonder when you passed all the other ones. You may get a start and think you hadn't been concentrating to allow those junctions to go unnoticed. You may analyse the state of your mind to have allowed that? I can assure you, most of those times, you had allowed the chatter in your mind to quieten and your unconscious mind was safely in control.

When you practice your diaphragmatic breathing, you may find yourself releasing any tensions you may have been feeling. The more you breathe deeply the easier it is to settle into such a relaxed state that your mind no longer chatters thus giving you the freedom to work with your unconscious mind. Take this opportunity of 'speaking' with your unconscious mind. Ask it things like, 'Unconscious mind if its for my highest good, please give me 3, 4 or 5 (you choose the number) solutions to defeat/control my fear of flying. Please give them to me over the next …… (give a time scale, ie 3 days, week et cetera). Ask your unconscious mind to give you assistance to collapse your fear of flying and to collapse your anticipatory pattern leading up to your flight.

Thank your unconscious mind for its help and support, then take a deep breath and come back into the room. Shake your body. Drink lots of water and get on with your day or night without giving any further thought to your personal session. Its important to release any thoughts about your request because that will allow your chattering conscious mind to take over defeating the whole process. Its takes practice so please stick to it?

I have to add here – even the most sceptical of people have appreciated the benefits of this exercise of conversing with their unconscious mind - because it works.

Obviously having someone to facilitate your hypnosis creates better outcomes, however, with practice you should still notice a difference in your thinking pattern.

Squash the negatives and turn them into positives

Sit comfortably with your cupped hands outstretched in front of you, approximately shoulder width apart. You can bend your elbows if you find that more comfortable but resist leaning on anything.

In one cupped hand and using your imagination or visualisation put all the positive components of a successful experience you have had in the past, and really focus on filling that cup.

Add all the colours, sounds, scents, feelings you had.

In the other cup, put your anxiety of flying into it and see it all there, lying in your cupped hand. What does it look like? Feel like? Does it taste or sound of anything?

Take a deep breath, exhale slowly, centre yourself and return your focus onto your 'positive' cup and really amp up all the good things about that successful experience. And amp it up again until your hand is brimming with these positive components.

Back to your other hand, but this time – bring some component of your 'positive' experience cup to this negative one – and amp up the positive. In other words, what component or experience from that successful time can you bring to your negative hand that would overcome an aspect of your anxiety? It doesn't need to be huge, but just enough to chip away at that negativity.

Continue transferring the positive components to your negative cup, each time noticing that your negative cup is reducing in content – it may only be by a minute amount, just keep working at it. Some clients have found actually talking about what they're transferring helps, so it may with you too.

Continue from hand to hand (taking a deep breath in and out as you go from each hand) until there is little to nothing left of the negatives.

You may well find your hands have gradually become closer to each other.

When your hands are almost touching - Quickly clasp your hands together – squashing any remaining negativity out and all the positivity in.

For a few moments hold your hands together like this and breathe deeply. Allow any energy produced by the exercise to fill your body – actually *feel* it and relish it.

You may get extra strength by taking your clasped hands up to your heart space and by opening your hands press all the healthy positives into your chest.

Release and get on with something else.

Please don't hurry this exercise and allow the benefit of it to really take shape.

Flick the Switch

Here's another little exercise you can do that will give you surprising but quite powerful results. Its an exercise I do with my clients. –

Find yourself a quiet place, where you won't be disturbed. Switch your phone off, make sure you are comfortable and start your deep breathing. Sit or lie comfortably but with your hands resting by your sides, hands relaxed but fingers open - not touching.

As you relax into your breathing, think of a memory of a happy time in your life. A time when everything went so right you could almost high 5 yourself right now just thinking about it. Then amp up the colours surrounding this time, the sounds, the positive, happy feelings. Build up this memory to a peak in your mind, and when you reach that peak (you will find it with repetitive practice), press your thumb and any finger tightly together, or hold your thumb, or grip your wrist –

always use the same place each time because you are *anchoring* that feel good feeling into your system.

Release your hold and let the power of the memory fade, in other words – turn the sound down.

Repeat the process again, only this time really amp it up, see the colours even brighter, sounds even more clearly, feelings experienced, was there a particular smell attached to this memory? Taste? If so, amp them up too, take it up another notch, and another – press your anchor point to lock in those feelings, and thoughts into your mind.

Release your hold and relax.

Give yourself some minutes into your relaxation then press your anchor point again. Can you feel the power return to your mind and body? As with most skills in life, this exercise takes practice and maintenance. Maintenance as in a well-oiled, cared for engine in peak condition, ready to fire up with the flick of a switch.

This exercise teaches you to 'anchor' the feel good feelings firmly into your mind so that in times when you need to have the power instantly to transcend or control anxiety, all you do is grip where you set the anchor on your body and breathe.

Again, practice constantly so that you have a powerful measure of positive determination flood your mind and body when you need it.

A simple 5 part exercise to deal with Anxiety Rushes

(Formally called Panic Attacks)

ADRENAL GLANDS

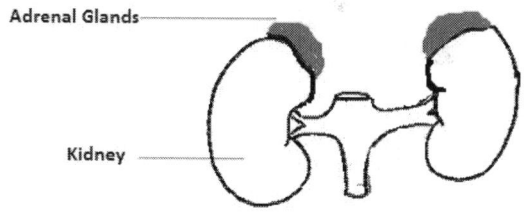

Diagram not to scale

What Is an Anxiety Rush?

Firstly, understand that anxiety rushes are so common that there are probably people around you in a crowd – shopping, eating, walking, at a ball game – wherever – right now who are suffering from an anxiety rush.

Its your body's way of protecting you from possible harm. The message of 'fear', or 'beware' or just plain 'warning' flashes a signal to your adrenal glands to warn of danger. They then kick in by releasing adrenalin into your system to allow you a 'fight or flight' reaction. They're GOOD. They look after you. They are not to be despised or cursed.

HOWEVER, this extra dose of adrenalin coursing through your body and not being used up in a fight or flight situation can become a terrible experience of thinking you're having a heart attack, or you're going to die from lack of oxygen, or…….. you're just going to look plain stupid to strangers. How do you explain that one to people, even your nearest and dearest?

The thing is – as long as the adrenalin is allowed to flow through your bloodstream with nowhere to go – so the anxiety rush will seem to last for ever, and it will appear to be completely out of your control. The greater your anxiety – MORE adrenalin will be produced and pumped through your system until it's in overload...and THAT'S what you're left trying to deal with.

Now here's an interesting fact. – It can take approximately as little as 3 minutes for this situation to develop. During that time, your heart is pumping extra hard to deal with the excess doses of adrenalin. It can do the job – but in the meantime – its a scary feeling for the person going through it.

Once your brain stops warning the body that there's danger – the adrenal glands stop producing and pumping adrenalin into your system.

So the trick is – to stop the production of that adrenalin going overboard. And by using these exercises you can stop an anxiety rush before it starts and handle just a few minutes of reaction.

Its THAT simple. Of course, the more you do these exercises the quicker and easier the response, and pretty soon you've trained yourself to have no more anxiety rushes.

Tip. – If anxiety rushes are a recurring problem for you, ie having to face the same things over and over again – I suggest you write your simple exercises on a palm card, or piece of cardboard, so that you can focus on them and go through them in a more ordered fashion. Keep it with you all the time, or have several in different places. One really good place is in your wallet/purse, another near your phone, and so on. Read through them frequently so that you're better prepared for 'the real thing'. Trust them like your best friend – treat them as such. If you're quietly sitting having a coffee – get your card out and go through the exercises in that moment of relaxation. Remember. – Practice makes perfect. And the more you use them – the quicker the results and effects. You want to get to that stage when you no longer need to look at your card – all the information is stored in your brain.

The Five Simple Steps to control anxiety rushes:

Remind yourself that you are simply on the *verge* of an anxiety rush AND you can handle it.

Nothing more serious is happening. You can contain it and it will be over in minutes.

Diaphragmatic Breathing – take a deep breath, filling your stomach with air so that it pushes outwards, and as you exhale say under your breath 'relax' or 'release' or 'steady' or 'strength' – any word similar to these should have the bigger impact for you. Repeat this breathing, but this time breathe in for a count of 4, hold your breath for a count of 3, exhale for count of 5. Repeat again so that you've taken 3 deep breaths. Continue to concentrate on your diaphragmatic breathing throughout.

Stop the fear from rising by shouting in your mind 'STOP' loudly or seeing a 'STOP' sign in your mind. This interrupts the negative message to the adrenal glands before you get swamped with adrenalin. Often your mind works in a 'loop' of negative thoughts and messages. This STOP – will shut down the loop before it gets out of control.

Immediately put your attention onto a positive coping message, ie 'I'm not having a heart attack.' 'I am safe.' 'I will not die.' 'I will work my way out of this – now.' 'I'll be fine in 3/4/5 minutes.' 'Breathe.' 'Centre (use your name here).' Be firm with these commands.

Or statements like – 'I've brought myself through this situation so many times before and I will get through it this time.'

'I am fine, everything is fine.' Repeat your statement/s as often as you need.

Validate your feelings. Don't minimise them. See them for what they are and what they represent, and how you can adapt these exercises to be even more effective next time. Look for the 'trigger' that sets these rushes off and deal with that. And truly believe that the more you do these exercises the more 'in control' you will become, therefore you will feel even stronger and more able to cope. You are taking control of your reactions/experiences/situations. You are breaking the pattern to your anxiety.

Finally, congratulate yourself. Even if you felt you could have done better (hindsight is a wonderful thing.) still give yourself a pat on your back – you did well.

'Stop!' The Media

Because you suffer from this fear, you are automatically predisposed to noticing and reading/watching negative stories about flying/aircraft; which in turn, attach and feed the fear. Newspapers in particular love to up the fear stakes with lurid and highly descriptive photographs/films. If these instances were regular – do you think anyone would print it or report it? They just wouldn't be 'news' would they? Ignore. Its not going to help you and there is nothing you can do about any air incidences anyway. Also be politely wary of scare stories from other people as there is often some exaggeration which is a human frailty.

A good exercise to turn these negatives into positives? Each time you feel drawn towards these stories, shout 'stop.' silently in your mind and immediately hum a tune, sing, look at something else – do anything to distract your attention, and then...........congratulate yourself on successfully ignoring the story. Bit by bit you will wean yourself off the compulsion and replace it with feelings of being in control.

Rather, tune into positive stories about flights/flying – ones that contain facts.

I take back control of my mind and body.

EFT or Emotional Tapping Technique

EFT has its basis in Chinese acupuncture and psychology but instead of using needles, a sequence of fingertip 'tapping' on particular meridian points on the upper body is used. EFT is a painless, surprisingly simple yet a recognised and highly effective method of stress management, generating energy and positivity in a variety of areas and situations. Extensive research has validated EFT with critical reviews published in the American Psychological Association's (APA) journal *Review of General Psychology,* among other authoritive bodies. And in case anyone wonders if EFT produces a placebo effect, a study published in the *Energy Psychology Journal* confirmed that the benefits from EFT are as a result of the tapping process. Enjoy the simplicity of this exercise which can be used for any situation/issue.

Diagram:

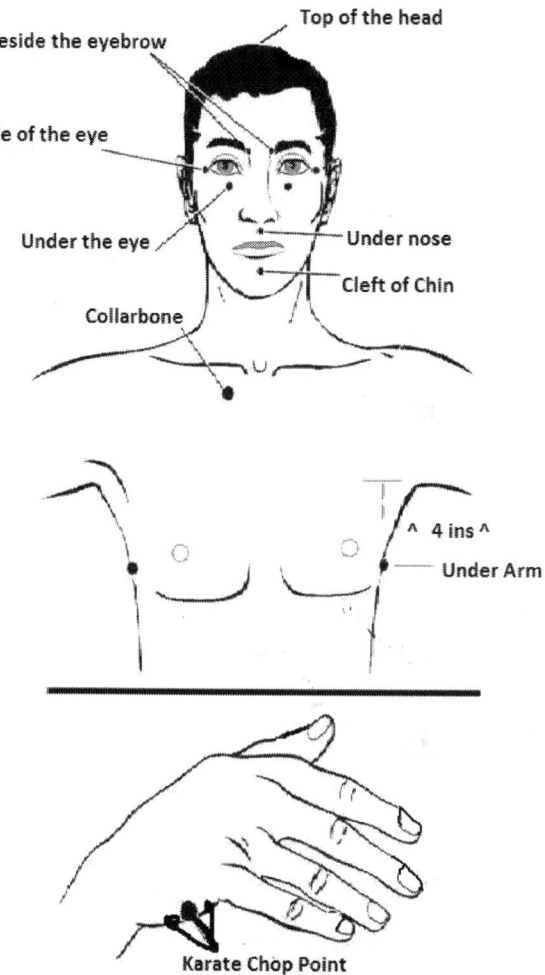

Method:

Sit comfortably straight. Feet flat on floor. With your back supported.

Take a couple of Diaphragmatic breaths.

On a scale of 1 to 10 – (1 being the least, 10 being the most) judge your reaction to whatever concerns you to tap on and put that number on the scale. For instance, flying. On a scale of 1 to 10 how do you feel about flying? And put that number on your scale.

(The object of the scale is to show you through progression that the feeling of anxiety lessens).

Spend a short moment to think about it. Know you are in safe surroundings and this is simply an exercise to clear the anxiety/negativity/stress et cetera to allow for clarity of thinking, control and lessening the stress/impact you're feeling about a certain situation/issue.

Diaphragmatic breath (deep, slow breath filling your lungs and diaphragm)

Using the four fingers of one hand as shown on the diagram -

Start tapping your karate chop point, and say - "Even though I....................(whatever - your choice and word) for example, "Even though I am anxious about flying" or "Terrified" or "Scared witless!" (This is your phobia remember so use words that are pertinent to you and how you feel).

"I deeply,

"And completely,

"Accept myself." (or 'accept my .... whatever you're tapping for)

Repeat at least twice both movement and words

Then move onto the points shown on the face of the diagram. Using your index and middle finger on either hand but consistently use that hand throughout the sequence, tap each point at least 5 or more times. Saying at the same time as tapping "I accept my ...." at each point, starting with –

- Top of your head – 'I accept my...............'
- Inner eyebrow – 'I accept my...................'
- Beside your eye – 'I accept my................'

- Under your eye - 'I accept my................'
- Under your nose - 'I accept my................'
- In the cleft of your chin - 'I accept my................'
- Collarbone - 'I accept my................'
- Under your arm (approximately 3 to 4 inches from your armpit) - 'I accept my................'

When you finish the sequence take a deep breath.

You have now truly come to terms with your fear. By recognising it, you may now tap to reduce/defeat it.

Check where you are on your scale of 1 to 10.

Repeat with:

Tapping on your karate chop point say,

- 'Even though I'm frightened of flying, I deeply and completely accept myself.
- 'Even though I'm frightened of flying, I deeply and completely accept myself.

- 'Even though I'm frightened of flying, I deeply and completely accept myself."

Moving to tap on the top of your head and proceed with the sequence, saying with each point, from there to under your arm – remember to tap each point at least 5 times.

- Tap top of your head and say, "I accept I'm afraid of flying".

- Eyebrow point – "I accept that I'm afraid of flying but I'm working on that."

- Side of the eye – "I know if I work on my fear, it will no longer hurt me."

- Under the eye – "I am taking charge of this now."

- Under the nose – "This fear has taken away too much of me and I will no longer let it."

- Chin – "I am willing to let go of this fear because it does me no good."

- Collarbone – "I allow feelings of strength to take its place."

- Under the arm – "I am feeling stronger about flying already."

When you finish the sequence take a deep breath.

Check where you are on your scale of 1 to 10.

Continue your tapping until you reach a 1 or 2 on your scale which is minimal yet realistic, even a 3 is okay. Adapting your script each time towards this aim.

For example:

- Head - 'I know I have the tools and strength to beat this'
- Eyebrow - 'I can feel the shift happening and I am stronger'
- Side of eye - 'I am in control now'
- Under nose - 'I relish this feeling of control'
- Chin - 'I am in control and I look forward to flying'
- Collarbone - 'I have defeated the fear, it is gone'

- Under arm – 'I am proud of myself'

Take a couple of diaphragmatic breaths and relax. I advise you then to go and do something knowing that you are feeling much better. Don't sit and dwell or analyse – it could negate your good work.

Adapting the script to suit, and changing the words as you go through the sequence is a vital part of this process. Its important to start with the negative to recognise it, after all – it exists. Then gradually through the tapping process, turn it into a positive – ie I can release this/I am free of this/I am confident of moving forward, I know I can fly and so on.

If you practice this exercise diligently you will still be able to bring up in your mind and body the wellbeing benefits by simply repeating the exercise in your head with no actions. Or sometimes just tapping your karate chop point on your knee or arm of your chair, or even on your steering wheel, the tray in front of you on a plane, or the arm of your chair, and you will benefit from the whole exercise without appearing odd or obvious if out with people or in crowds. (Something I've noticed quite recently – there are a lot of people tapping out there – I've seen it and smiled).

There are good free videos on the internet to refer to. I recommend Nick Ortner on www.thetappingsolution.com

Roll Play

Some of you may find the simple game of 'role play' useful. A good time for this is while you're waiting to board – imagine yourself to be someone different. For example, a famous sportsman/woman about to fly to an Awards Ceremony where you'll be given an award for your lifetime successes to sport. What will you wear? Will you have to go shopping beforehand for the perfect outfit? How will you prepare for the ceremony? What will you say to the reporters waiting for your arrival at the airport for photos and comments? What make and colour is the limo taking you to the awards? Is there a red carpet? How red is the carpet? Which celebrities, famous people, people you admire – will be there and ready to shake your hand, hug you, speak with you? How will you respond to the congratulations/respect shown to you, what will you say when given the award, how will you celebrate? And so on. You can substitute sportsman/woman to any role you wish because after all – it is your wish, your fantasy, your movie. (This exercise can be really good if travelling with children. You don't want to pass on your fears so engaging them in your fantasy can make you more determined to stick to it and also, becoming involved in their roles too can focus your attention on the game and away from negative anticipation of getting on the plane.)

Visualisation

Simple exercise - but it works. Try it for yourself right now. Read this scenario then sit quietly, take a deep breath, and imagine it all.

You're feeling thirsty. Visualise standing up and going through to your kitchen. Reach for a glass. Where do you keep them? Visualise that clearly. Hold your glass up to the light – what does it look like? Does it have a pattern or is it clear? Is it warm or is it cold? Feel the temperature of that glass.

Turn on the cold water tap. Can see you see the water flowing from the tap into the basin? What does it look like? Can you smell it? Can you hear it gurgling down the plug-hole?

Run your fingers under the water, is it cold enough to drink? If it is – fill your glass. Then visualising all the details of your kitchen, the glass, the water, the tap, your actions – lift the glass up to your lips. Does it have a smell attached to it? What does it smell like? Then – take a drink of that water. Can you feel the coolness of it? Taste the freshness?

Were you able to visualise that whole action of getting yourself a glass of water to quench your thirst?

Visualisation is a cognitive technique to help you achieve what you want with greater ease and confidence.

A well-known and cited example of this technique is attributed to the experiment by Australian Psychologist Alan Richardson. To test his theory of the very real effects of Visualisation or Mental Imagery, he invited a group of basketball students to participate in his experiment by making – I believe – 100 basketball shots into the hoop.

He then randomly divided those players – who incidentally had no experience of visualisation – into three groups.

He had one group 'A' practice throws into the hoop for 20 minutes every day, 5 days every week for 4 weeks.

He had the second group 'B' practice throwing the basketball into the hoop on the 1st day of his experiment and again on the 28th day of the experiment but with no further practice of throwing basketballs in between those two designated days.

The third group 'C' were directed to come to the court for 20 minutes, 5 days a week. He told them that they would be guided by a professional in visualizing to shoot goal shots, not physically shoot them, in fact, without even touching a ball.

After 4 weeks Richardson had the subjects shoot 100 goal shots again.

Group A had improved in their ability by 24%.

Group B made no significant improvement.

Group C - the group guided in visualisation, improved their goal scoring by 23%. Only 1% less than the group who physically practiced the most.

In his paper on the experiment, published in Research Quarterly, Richardson wrote that the most effective visualisation occurs when the person visualising feels and sees what he is doing. In other words, the visualisers in the basketball experiment "felt" the ball in their hands and "heard" it bounce, in addition to "seeing" it go through the hoop.

This is just one example of the effects and results of repetitive 'visualisation' of the many documented experiments and/or best practises. There are so many other examples that you may have noticed, for instance, golfers lining up to putt, rugby players preparing to kick the ball over the posts. Even equine people walk courses not only to familiarise themselves with the obstacles they have to take a horse over, but also so they can map out the course in their minds and how they'll play it.

If you are determined to set aside as little as 10 minutes a day to sit quietly and 'visualise' getting on a plane and flying, you will notice significant and positive results. This is 'brain training', fixing that its okay to fly into your unconscious mind, so that when the time comes to fly – you'll be doing it with a whole different mind-set. Try it, stick to it, and see?

Get connected

Whenever you see a plane flying overhead, take a moment to watch it. Visualise being on it. Go through your exercises as you do. Check your breathing and make it deeper. Tap your karate chop point, Flick the Switch. If your mind spins into trying to stop yourself from performing these exercises, preferring instead to linger on negative thoughts, shout STOP in your mind. Visualise and roleplay. Imagine the people in the plane. Are they being served food right now? Where do you think they'll be going and why? Bring in your roleplay – in an ideal world – what would you be doing right now up there, excited about your destination...... and so on.

If someone tells you they've booked a flight, watch your language and thoughts, demolish the negative ones and replace with positive ones. Instead of saying things like, 'Oh you're so lucky you're not afraid.' Concentrate on replacing it with, 'Oh you're so lucky. I wish I was going.' or 'I'm so looking forward to my next flight whenever it is.' Get connected. You are training your brain to be positive about flying. It helps.

Mental Dialogue

To review, "Sticks and stones can break my bones, but words can never harm me." Experience tells us that in actual fact – words can break you – harsh, negative words can certainly break you. Its 'who' is saying the words that can really undo you. If it's another person, you have a choice. You can either rebut them, ignore them, or keep silent (but mentally clobber them). Which of these options feel better to use?

But - what do you do when your harshest critic is...........yourself? You know what I mean, that little voice that demolishes your positive intentions, plans, ideas, before they become actions. The one that says, '*You kidding? You really think you should do that? Isn't it better to live with what you know without changing things? You think you're good enough for that?'* And so, you listen to that voice and with a heave of regret – do/say nothing and revert back to 'normal'. But does that silence that inner critic? No, your mental conversation then clings to, *'why didn't I...........'*

So what can you do about this? Firstly, begin to change your actual language. Instead of saying, *'I can't because...........'* change that to a qualifier. For example, *'I can't right now, and right now, I will work on changing that.'*

A really good exercise to 'change' language is to read some media report of an issue with negative dialogue. As in find a headline (not to do with planes, flying, airports, or anything remotely related to flying). Something that you can dissemble. Read the headline, then read the article. Does the headline accurately represent the article or is it exaggerated? How would you change that headline to comfortably fit in with the article? Admittedly your headline wouldn't sell the newspaper, magazine or whatever but it will allow you to notice the power of words and the power they have over your attention.

If you *have* to read a story about a plane incident, read it analytically. Break down what is being reported, highlight assumptions, note how long in time the story is strung out. How much is theory, opinion, speculation? Ask yourself – is this information truly informative or can I discard it? And use your exercises for example 'tap' it away with EFT to firmly discard it and release any interest in it or prevent from becoming an attachment.

Modelling

'Modelling' is a basic tenet of NLP – Neuro-Linguistic Programming. Simply put – it suggests you find a good role model and copy their behaviour. The more you do this, the more chance you have of changing your thought pattern to work more positively and in your favour. There must be someone around or close to you, who enjoys flying. Someone who feels excited at the very thought of planes and flying – *copy* them. Copy their speech, bearing, words and actions – the whole deal. Add some 'mirror work' to this, by practicing in front of a mirror. Heck, go the whole hog and roleplay it too. Be BIG in your reflection. And if anyone's watching be even bigger in your representation – have fun with it. (If you have a reaction of laughter at this performance – let it happen. Laughter is a great reliever).

Triggers

Work to recognise your 'triggers', those little things that put you into a mind-set of anxiety. Analyse their legitimacy. In other words – what do you need to do to demolish them? Write all those triggers down in your diary/notebook. Score through any that really hold no validity and work through the rest – scoring them off each time you have demolished them, or better still – replace them with positive action. This is also a 'visual' exercise that you can refer back to to take stock of your power to diminish/demolish and know you can do the same with other areas of your life.

Support Network

I believe you'll achieve quicker, longer lasting results if you build a network of like-minded people and people who want to help you. There are various forums online and Facebook for support and encouragement, and I am developing my own forum and would hope you'd become an active member of it – information on my website www.welcomecoaching.com

Symbolic action

Some people like to perform a tangible action to release their fear. An example of which is to write on a piece of paper the words, "I release and banish my fear of flying. To be free of it once and for all."

Burn that piece of paper (and please take adequate steps to do this safely) and release the ashes of it into the air, never to return in solid form.

If you prefer not to burn it, put it into your freezer and freeze it out.

VAKOG

VAKOG is an NLP representational system which I am adapting here to give you yet another tool with which to help you and understand yourself better.

Basically, VAKOG represents the five human sensory representations. In the NLP world we agree that most people have a predominant 'sense' and VAKOG is a basic 'model' or 'modality' used extensively by NLP practitioners in determining which 'sense' our client uses to express themselves internally and externally. (This creates an almost instant rapport because it allows the practitioner to use the client's 'language').

Notice the words below, which do you mostly use? Can you identify your 'sense'?

V – visual: look, see, watch, notice, focus, imagine, visualise, perspective, reflect, clarify

A – auditory: say, accent, tone, sound, deaf, ring, shout, listen, speechless, vocal, silence

K – kinaesthetic: touch, handle, contact, push, rub, solid, tackle, push, pressure, feel

O – olfactory: smell, scented, stale, fishy, nosy, fragrant, smoky, fresh

G – gustatory: taste, bitter, sweet, sour, mouth

Adapting this information to give you an aid with which to help you, try this-

If you are:-

Visually led – take with you happy photos, or any 'picture' that makes you happy. Colouring in books are good too.

Auditory led – take headphones with your favourite music or programmes

Kinaesthetic – stress balls or something similar is good, colouring-in books, origami sets with instructions and papers, something to do with your hands

Olfactory – use small drops of perfume or essential oils to sniff. I usually put these on the cuff on my sleeve so that if I want to fall asleep I can tuck my hand under my cheek and breathe it in to my heart's content. Check for bespoke essential oils from my recommended aromatherapist under the heading Aromatherapist in next chapter – 'Supporting Aids' page 39

Gustatory – Lollypops are good. Anything that gives you satisfaction whilst sucking/chewing – also helps prevents your ears popping during take-offs and landings due to a change in cabin air pressure.

Focus on your destination not your flight

Instead of focusing on counting down the time until you board - count down the time until you arrive. I know this can seem pretty simple, but sometimes the simple things are very powerful if you are determined. You see, when we focus on something significant, we mentally attach similar things to it, ie memories, experiences, et cetera and if its negative thinking - we become overwhelmed not surprisingly, and that's when the 'fight or flight' reflex is triggered. It's your mind and body trying to protect you. Tip – as soon as you board, if you're flying to another time zone – change your watch to that time zone.

Inflight relaxation, calming aid

Most airlines are aware of nervous passengers and provide specific channels on the inflight entertainment modules for added comfort. This can take the form of calming music, guided meditations, articles and exercises in their inflight magazines et cetera, use them. They are also an endorsement that airlines do understand they carry nervous passengers.

My plane is a no smoke zone

Some nervous flyers think that not being able to smoke on a plane will make them feel worse – think again. If you are a smoker, use the diaphragmatic breathing exercises as a replacement as it is considered that it is the deep breathing used in smoking that actually has the calming effect on you, not the nicotine and chemicals.

Change your fear to curiosity

Change your fear to curiosity. Become informed because *knowledge is power*.

And know one other very important point – it takes real courage to admit, work on and defeat your anxiety. Honour that because it contains a strength that many don't have.

In the past you may have looked at other passengers with some envy at the ease they have with flying. But – who is the one who is courageous enough to get on that plane and fly in the first place?

I do firmly believe that your fear has its roots in an occasion or incident that took place when you were too young, or in a vulnerable state of mind, or inexperienced or lacking the knowledge to deal with it effectively. It may have involved you, or you may have been witness to it. It need not have been a major incident, but it had enough of an impact that it created the roots of your issue.

Whatever caused or created your anxiety, please don't try to banish it by pushing it away or burying it in the hope it will magically go away. All that will do is to keep it in your mind, lurking in the background ready to spring into action and remind you it's still there – often when you are least able to deal with it. You may of course already realise this, for in the past you have tried to avoid it or banish it only to find it returning time and again to haunt you.

Instead become curious. Learn whatever you can about planes, flights, and anything associated with flying, and I mean – facts – not speculations or opinions – but FACTS.

Desensitise your sensitivity.

Get rid of your panic buttons that spark off your anxiety by recognising what they are and demolishing them.

NEVER denigrate yourself. Don't use negative words to describe or reason or excuse your fear. Each time you think or say something like, "I can't get on a plane. Millions do, why not me? I feel so weak. I just don't want to. I'm too scared." - *alert* - say it often enough, you will be giving your unconscious mind the commands that you *are* weak and that you don't want to get on that plane. That's what you've said, and probably often enough for your unconscious mind to accept and help you to – stay safe and *not* get on that plane. You've given it an order and it will go into action to deliver that order by providing solutions to – not getting on that plane. Train your mind to be determined to fly – and you will have a strong ally to help you win and be free of the fear.

Please note –

It is entirely probable that one course of action or exercise to eradicate your fear will not work on another person. It may also be the case that one exercise will not work entirely either. This is because each of us has a fear that is unique to us. The initial reason, with the added attachments makes it unique so it does follow that the solution to this complex thought pattern is a combination of aids. So...........

Work on the exercises I've given you to the best of your ability, especially the diaphragmatic breathing which lays down a healthy foundation. Please give each exercise a good effort. Choose the ones that work well with you and prioritise them. I advise that you create a daily routine of performing these exercises – there is after all no lasting 'quick fix'. It stands to reason that it took considerable time to develop the fear in the first place, so too it will take time and patience to defeat it. Keep notes in your diary to refer back to – always helps. Don't completely give up on any one exercise though, because you are going through a progressive programme of evolving into a happy flyer. I have given you a variety of exercises to give you choice.

Other Fears and phobias

Some people have other phobias, such as claustrophobia or a fear of heights. And *these* fears and reactions are their dominant concern rather than a fear of flying. Their worry is that by being in a plane can set off a panic attack or in less extreme cases – lead to an uncomfortable, stressful flight.

In my world – a phobia is a phobia. Although each client is unique, their fears still generally originate in the same way, and emanate in the same pattern therefore the same exercises as I've given for aerophobics do and will - work with these other phobias.

I recognise my fear, I am resolving it, I am willing to release it to set myself free.

SUPPORTING AIDS

Music to calm jangled nerves

I've been very lucky over the years to discover and use the beautiful and calming music of two very talented musicians/composers for clients and my own listening pleasure. I am therefore very happy to recommend them to you to help calm you and give you feelings of peace.

Terry Oldfield and Christopher Lloyd Clarke have been composing, playing and recording their music for many years to international acclaim, and I advise playing their music as background to your exercises because when you are in a situation of simply listening to it, your unconscious mind will connect the music to your exercises giving you the beneficial experience of calm and control. Of course, you can listen to this music any time to just relax and chill out.

Terry Oldfield creates music that I have listened to for many years. Its soothing, beautiful and very easy to relax to under any circumstance. I have used it sometimes to fall asleep because I know it will always produce lovely dreams. His compositions are both uplifting and calming and I highly recommend him to you.

To quote the introduction of Terry on his website

Terry Oldfield is a world renowned musician best known for his unique style of flute playing. He has been nominated for a British Academy award and two Emmy awards during his career and has composed music for over 80 Film and Television productions, receiving two Emmy nominations for "Land of the Tiger" and "Twilight of the Dreamtime" and also a British Academy Award nomination as composer for the BBC series "Kingdom of the Ice Bear". Copyright Terry Oldfield

You can download his works and discover more about Terry, his music, retreats and tours from his website
https://terryoldfield.com/

Christopher Lloyd Clarke produces the very music I use in the background of my therapy sessions, and my two recorded hypno works – 'Steps to Freedom' to release people from obsolete emotional weights, and 'Labour of Love' a recording for pregnant women.

To quote the introduction of Christopher on his website –

Christopher Lloyd Clarke creates music for deep relaxation, healing and enhanced meditation. From his studio in Torquay, Australia, his ongoing mission is to create music that helps people live happier, healthier and more peaceful lives.

Copyright Christopher Lloyd Clarke

Christopher has a wide range of his music on his website, and can be sampled before you buy.

To listen to his music and learn more about him, please go to

http://www.christopherlloydclarke.com/

Both of these remarkable men have put their hearts into their music and that comes across when you listen to them. I recommend them above all others and very happy they allowed me to include them in this book for you.

Nutrition

It may appear to be a little odd to add what you eat and drink to a support position, but it does play a very valid role in how you feel, how you anticipate your flight and how you manage yourself during your flight.

Dawn Swinley is a highly regarded nutrition expert based in England, here is her advice:

Having been cabin crew and now a nutritional therapist I know only too well that food and drink can affect you and your mood especially when flying.

Symptoms that are typically associated with flying are dehydration and gastrointestinal discomfort because gases expand when you're in the air.

Feeling anxious? Then avoid caffeine and alcohol. I recommend you reduce your caffeine intake a few days prior your journey.

Avoid fizzy drinks, onions, garlic, potatoes, dairy products and beans as these are all gas producing foods.

Avoid processed and fried foods, sugary items and white bread as these make you feel tired, unsettled and unsatisfied.

Drink water before and during the flight add lemon or lime to it. Consuming fruit is also a good source of hydration. Move about the cabin especially if it's a long haul flight.

Foods that can help anxiety include whole grains, seaweed, blueberries, Acai berries, almonds, chocolate, Maca root.

Foods containing magnesium, vitamin B12 (and other B vitamins), zinc and antioxidants can be beneficial for helping you deal with stress. There are also herbal supplements like kava and passionflower.

Drink mint, chamomile tea as these soothe the stomach and take a probiotic daily as this helps regulate the digestive system.

Setting your watch to your destination time zone mentally prepares you; physically you act, sleep and eat accordingly which helps jetlag.

The name Mode de Vie means "way of life" and in this instance it means a simpler, healthier and more fun "way of life" for YOU.

That's what I'm all about. I'm a nutritional therapist known as The Drop a Dress Size I. I specialize in helping midlife women who want to lose that stubborn belly fat, increase their energy levels, maintain their weight and get their Mojo back.

My work is about life balance, not faddy diets or yo-yo dieting (as we know this is not the answer) but it's about your mindset, nutrition and moving your body. I believe in the 80/20 rule and we are what we eat. So by changing a few bad habits, eating for your metabolism and enjoying your food one step at a time you will achieve and maintain your goals.

My practice is in Gloucester, England - but I support clients nation and worldwide. I also offer workshops, online programmes, Skype appointments and webinars.

Change is not easy. Knowing what to do is one thing. Implementing it is a whole other matter. This is where I come in.

www.mode-de-vie.co.uk
All Copyrights Dawn Swinley

Aromatherapy

Is a useful aid, to help calm you and relieve you from the 'stale air' of a pressurised cabin. A colleague of mine is a highly respected Clinical Aromatherapist who can make up bespoke preparations for you. Jane Lawson is based in England and has clinics throughout England; she also uses Skype for personal one-to-one sessions. She will make up an Essential Oil specifically for you incorporating not only the scents you would benefit from with your fear, but also other personal-to-you scents for a whole value added benefit.

This is what Jane has to say to you.

> *My Name is Jane Lawson. I am known as a 'Vintage' Clinical Aromatherapist, 25 years time served! I am also Principal and Founder, Therapist and Teacher based in Gloucester, but also available in Fleetwood, Cambridge, Derby, Coventry, Halstead, Manchester and Chiswick, London.*

Specialist areas:

Clinical Aromatherapy. Clinical Reflexology, Metamorphic Technique, Reiki, Touch For Health (Kinesiology), KaHuna Massage. Touch Finger Therapy (TM), Past Life Therapy, ESR.

Some 17 years ago I was accredited to teach both Aromatherapy and Clinical Aromatherapy and Reflexology.

Over the years I started looking at essential oils in a wholly different way and found a much simpler and easier way to determine which Essential Oil is best suited to treat what ails folk. The chemistry of Essential Oils is very important, but to the lay person and many therapists it can be very confusing when reading all the various 'directories' that are available. So my company and clinic The Natural Approach to Essential Oils was born.

To reduce your fear of flying, I can make up a bespoke essential oil just for you. Please contact me for details and no obligation discussions via phone, email, Skype, in person.

<u>www.thenaturalapproach.biz</u>
Copyright Jane Lawson

On-board Stretches and exercises

I suggest you practice these stretches/exercises prior to any flight so that you have a good knowledge of their benefits. And instead of sitting tensely on a chair in the departure lounge, go through them whilst you wait. Working in conjunction with your breathing exercise, they will go a long way to preparing you to board your plane.

Please be aware of other passenger's space though when seated on-board. Exercise will allow you to feel more comfortable, and going through them will help you to positively focus on 'you'. They can be repeated as often as you feel you need them; do go through them though please.

Exercises to do in your seat on an aeroplane by Pip Deave MCSP, Chartered Physiotherapist Grad.Dip.Phys., MCSP, Dip. Inject Ther, APPI

1. Sit straight in your seat with your feet flat on the floor (or on a footrest, bag or folded blanket if your feet don't reach the floor). Put your hand on your tummy, just below your ribs and focus on your breathing. As you breathe in through your nose your tummy

should push your hand forward a little. Breathing out through your relaxed mouth (not pursed lips) should give you the feeling of your tummy pulling gently away from your hand. Continue for ten full breaths.

2. Breathe in again, and as you breathe out, squeeze your buttocks together as hard as you can and feel how your body will lift up a little. See how high you can lift your head to see what's going on in front of you.

3. Push your tail-bone into the back of the seat, arching your low back away from the seat. See if you can fit your hand in the space created behind your waist. Now tuck your tail underneath you, pushing your waist onto your hand and into the seat-back. Repeat several times. Perhaps after this you will feel you need a little more support in your low back – a cushion or rolled jumper may make you feel more comfortable.

4. Take a breath in and, as you breathe out, shrug your shoulders towards your ears and then bring them backwards and downwards as you inhale. Continue to roll your shoulders

backwards in this way for ten full breaths. Keep your shoulders in this down and back position for the next exercise.

5. Breathe in again and, as you breathe out, turn your head to the right as far as you can, as if looking at your neighbour. Return to the centre as you breathe in. Keep your body facing the front. Repeat from side to side three times, allowing your breathing to lead the movements.

6. Now take your right ear towards your right shoulder in the same way, feeling the stretch on the left side of the neck. Keep your shoulders down, hands on knees. Repeat either side three times.

7. Turn to the right as if looking behind you. Turn your whole body from your waist, pulling on your right armrest with your left hand to assist the movement. See if you can see the person behind you. Repeat both sides three times.

8. Lean forwards, taking your right hand towards the outside of your left ankle as if scratching your ankle or picking something up from the

floor. Repeat with the left hand reaching across to the outside of your right ankle. Three times each side.

9. Lean forwards with your forearms crossed on your knees. Maintain pressure on your knees whilst lifting both heels off the floor. Slowly lower your heels and then lift the fronts of your feet. Alternate heels lifting, toes lifting, slowly and as high as you can, pushing against the resistance of your weight leaning on your knees. Ten lifts to pump your calf muscles, improve circulation and prevent deep vein thrombosis.

10. Bend one knee up towards your chest, clasp your hands around your knee and pull gently towards you. Circle your ankle three times in each direction. Repeat with the other leg.

11. Reach one arm upwards towards the ventilation controls or overhead light. Stand up if you can or at least lift your bottom slightly off the seat as you stretch your arm. Repeat 3 times with each arm.

12. When you can, get up and walk down the aisle. Stand in the area behind the seats and

spend a few minutes going up and down on your toes, marching on the spot and stretching your arms and legs. Copyright Pip Deave All rights reserved

Pip qualified in 1982 at the Royal London Hospital and after gaining experience in several London hospitals and private practices she moved to the Forest of Dean, England in 1991. She started the Viney Hall practice in 1996. She has completed many post-graduate courses including gaining a Diploma in Injection Therapy in 1999 and in 2002 qualified as a Modified Pilates Teacher through the Australian Physiotherapy and Pilates Institute (APPI). Her experience, skills and straight talking have earned her an excellent reputation for sorting out physical problems that have proved difficult to help in the past. She enjoys leading the growing multidisciplinary team at Viney Hall and strives to maintain the high standards for which the clinic has become renowned.

www.vineyhallphysio.co.uk

Pamper not Punish

People who live with fears tend to punish themselves for them when, instead, recognition and nurturing have far better results. Ask yourself what 'punishing' yourself really achieves then reward yourself for realising it and deciding to change.

Yet, its all too easy to punish yourself for your 'failings' re flying but what good is that? Has that mental beating worked in the past? Has it encouraged you to get on a plane and fly? Instead, look to pampering yourself – and let's face it – on a flight there's plenty of time to do this.

Pampering can revive flagging spirits and reverse any personal negative feelings and thoughts. It makes you feel good and that can only enhance your flight as a nurturing experience. Looking after yourself by massaging creams and lotions on your face, arms, and hands has a calming, relaxing effect. And 'feeding' your skin to counteract the drying effects of cabin air not only gives you something rewarding to do but also helps to make you feel good which in turn, contributes to you viewing flying in a more positive frame.

I highly recommend Neal's Yard all natural products for ladies, men, children and babies. Neal's Yard Remedies can be found in most countries around the world, or can be ordered from Katie Chapman and Clare Bateman who recommend the following products:

Katie Chapman: A White Tea Face Mist, Frankincense Face Mask (trust me, great for keeping on while on a plane and it's clear so no-one needs to know!) and there's a new Oil-Free Hydrating Serum too that would be great. There's a 'Travel Remedy to Roll' too which is great for helping calm before flying...

Claire Bateman: I can second the frankincense face mask....it's a gel so you pop it on before you take off and away you go....I used it on our 6hr flight and my skin felt amazing

K Cox · I love the Wild Rose Beauty Balm for flights plus the relax/night time/travel Remedies to Roll (depending on the time of day). Before landing, I remove any excess balm, and use my other fave product - Frankincense Intense, and I also use the Frankincense Spritz for travels too. Beautiful products and those close to me on the plane / bus sometimes comment on the lovely aromas. There is a range of products for men, incl a moisturiser though my bf prefers to use the Frankincense Intense (this could be a bit rich for most men though). He likes the Bee Lovely lip balm for flights too, and the frankincense mist.

http://www.nealsyardremedies.com/
https://uk.nyrorganic.com/shop/katiechapman
http://uk.nyrorganic.com/shop/clairebateman

Motion Sickness

The bane of many travellers and one that is anticipated with anxiety. There are several things you can do to help yourself though.

In extreme cases, I'd advise a visit to your doctor for a prescription for this affliction. In lesser cases, your pharmacist will offer advice and products suitable to you. You may also pick up over the counter preparations in most airport shops/chemists.

More holistic methods can be used too, such as Motion Sickness Acupressure wrist straps which

I've personally found effective when flying through turbulence or as a passenger in a car going over rough terrain. These can be bought in chemists and department stores as well as online.

The aromatherapist I recommended will also make up an essential oil to aid you with motion sickness.

Stress Medication

If you have to resort to taking prescriptive medication, please make sure you get it through your doctor, and him/her when would be the best time to take it to be wholly effective. I'd suggest a dummy run a few days before your flight so that you can gauge its effects, as in - when it begins to take effect and how long it can last. Keep in mind you will probably be more anxious immediately prior to your flight and that may have an effect on its efficiency. Use the instructions carefully and please don't be tempted to take medication prescribed to someone else. FYI I used to take prescribed Diazepam because it would take the edge of my anxiety and also allowed me 2 to 4 hours sleep on-board.

There are natural preparations you can take. I highly recommend Bach Rescue Remedy, and the alcohol-free Rescue Remedy for my daughter when she was anxious about flying.

There are many such preparations in chemists, health-food shops, and online, I've just given you Bach Rescue Remedy because I've personally used it and found it to be easy to take and effective, and very handy to have in my bag. Neal's Yard Remedies produce an Australian Bush Flower Essence specifically for a fear of flying and it helps with travel fatigue too. Suppliers in Aids pages 41 and 44.

There are also 'teas' to help calm you, they can be found in natural food stores and supermarkets. Most are self-explanatory and teabags are convenient to take with you to drink during your flight. Please note that you may have to discard these tea bags prior going through Customs and Immigration in accordance to certain country's laws. Do check this thoroughly.

Flight Crew

Never forget your flight crew though. If you are feeling anxious – let them know. I've heard of so many instances whereby anxious passengers have quietly mentioned their fear to cabin crew and have been rewarded with support throughout the flight.

Laughter is a great 'aid' - seriously!

Watch comedies prior to your trip, in the departure lounge, and on the plane. Laughter releases those lovely chemicals called Endorphins, Serotonin and Dopamine which are known as 'feel-good' natural chemicals produced by your own body, and will lighten your thoughts thus releasing you from anxiety.

Instead of buying that heavy intellectual book you always meant to read but didn't really have the inclination (flyers will know what I mean), get one with humour. A book of jokes is a good one because you can dip in and out of it at whim.

I remember buying a book in the 1970s called 'Coffee, Tea or Me' written by an airhostess. It was of hilarious incidents/experiences this air hostess had during her years of flying. I read it on a flight from Melbourne to Perth and laughed all the way making the hours fly by (pardon unintentional pun). We had to stop at Adelaide to pick up more passengers and were allowed off the plane to 'stretch our legs'. Once on-board and in the air, I brought out my book again to read when I noticed the woman sitting across the aisle from me was reading 'Coffee, Tea or Me' too. She saw me looking, laughed and said, "You were having so much fun with that book that I had to get it too!" She'd bought it in the Transit Lounge Newsagents. Together we laughed our way to the end of our flight.

Check out my friend and Laughing Yogi – Joe Hoare www.joehoare.co.uk

Joe includes links to Youtube clips that will have you in stitches. Join his Newsletter and follow his blogs, they will certainly lighten you up and help with your anxiety. As he says, "Laugh about anything in life that isn't really funny".

Joe Hoare

My personal development work is about empowerment: helping people wake up, come

alive, be the best they can be, and enjoy the ride. Because this enjoyment is contagious, it gives others permission to enjoy the ride too. It stimulates qualities like connection & kindness, and its ultimate effect is to enhance people's experience of being alive, for the benefit of all.

I do this through courses, workshops, Retreats and one-to-one sessions. I do it however it works best, and find that the right people always attend the right session.

Professionally I have been running meetings, delivering conference sessions and providing workshops for over 30 years. My clients range from the international blue-chip companies (such as Kraft, Bank of Ireland, Novo Nordisk, Lloyds, Continental Airlines), to universities and colleges (including Bristol, Dundee, U.W.E, Cheltenham Science Festival), to charities and the Healthcare sector (Housing Associations, the NHS, Oxfam, NACTHPC, and others), and to the very experiential end of the spectrum like Glastonbury Festival. In 2006 I set up the UK's Laughter Facilitation course, to teach others how to use this material. *In 2000 I co-authored 'The Holistic*

Workspace', and in 2013 'Awakening the Laughing Buddha within' with the Barefoot Doctor.

I was a Director of the mould-breaking Pierian Centre in Bristol and am an occasional visiting lecturer at the University of the West of England in the fields of leadership, empowerment and health promotion.

I also trained in 'Laughter Yoga' with Dr Madan Kataria, founder of laughter clubs international, and run regular nls: natural laughter skills *sessions for organisations and the general public.*

My work regularly appears in the public eye, including BBC 2's 'Don't Die Young' with Dr Alice Roberts, the Johnny Walker Show on Radio 2, Points West, BBC 1's Inside Out, Discovery Health Channel, Radio 4, The Sunday Times, The Independent on Sunday, Nursing Times, Bristol Evening Post, among others.

In the late 1990's I ran BMA-accredited innovative stress management programmes.

http://www.joehoare.co.uk/
Copyright Joe Hoare

Aircraft Tracking

Some anxious passengers get relief from having someone 'track' their flight. I like to use this facility if any of my family or friends are flying. I mainly refer to www.flightradar24.com which is a brilliant site for tracking flights from departure gate to arrival gate. It's fascinating stuff and can actually become quite addictive – in the most positive way. The last time I used this tracking site was when my daughter and family were returning to Australia from the UK in 2015. There had been incursions in the Middle East at the time and I was relieved to watch their plane detour around this area. Yes, it added to their flight time a bit, but their safety was a priority to the airline.

Comforter/good luck charm

Think a 'comforter' or a good luck charm are just for babies and children? Think again. Anything that gives you that little bit 'extra' comfort is worth it and shouldn't be discounted. Having one of these with you can give you a psychological boost, and let's face it, anything that can help you not just get on a plane but enjoy it rather than endure it – is surely worth it?

Worry beads

Even a simple item like 'worry beads' can help you to relax. They were originally used by Greek Monks during prayers, however they have no religious meaning now and are used simply to relieve stress and promote relaxation. Worry beads are made from tactile substances, such as coral, amber, wood, or crystals, preferably not metal though. The more tactile they are, the better. The beads are strung along a hardy string with sufficient space to move the beads from one side to the next along the string and in one direction. The beads should be smooth and oval shape so they can slip through your fingers with ease. The sheer simplicity of this exercise is very calming. By progressively slowing the movement of beads your breathing may become more regulated and deeper, and your heart rate will begin to mimic the rhythm of the action. You can use one hand or both for this exercise and I suggest practicing either way just in case you are in a situation whereby you only have one hand free to use them.

Decongestants

You may find a small bottle of a decongestant such as Olbas Oil is useful to take onboard. Cabins with their pressurised air can become a bit stuffy and you may find a couple of drops of decongestant helps clear your breathing, which of course helps to calm you at the same time because you are drawing more oxygen into your lungs.

Apps

There are many apps to download on the internet which will help and support you. iTunes host some useful apps from Quantum Design Group.

I have support with any anxiety I may feel and I will ask for it.

FLYING DURING PREGNANCY, WITH BABIES OR YOUNG CHILDREN

I have included the following tips and information purely to lessen your stress levels. They are not completely conclusive to a flight but they may help you. Never hesitate to contact your airline with any questions you may have, it is also in their best interests to keep you a happy flier.

Pregnancy

Please check with your doctor, airline and insurance company for advice and regulations if you are pregnant. The only advice I give here is about your comfort to allow you to stress less.

Babies

Young babies can be surprisingly easy to fly with, particularly if you manage to book a 'skycot'. If you can't book a skycot or when travelling with young children request seats over the wing where there is less movement during any turbulence.

Don't take it for granted that airlines will provide you with everything required for a journey with your babe – the days of supplying you with nursery bags full of nappies, creams et cetera appear to be long gone. If you're using Formula you may want to take a couple of bottles of boiled water on-board with you – cafes and restaurants in departure areas are normally very kind to supply you with the boiled water if requested.

Always plan for delays where you may be sitting on the plane for longer than the departure time, which does happen. Usually due to a passenger arriving late.

For take-offs and landings, its generally a good idea to have your babe sucking on something, whether it be a dummy or bottle – something to work the muscles around the jaw to help to alleviate any pressure on their ears.

Medication

Unfortunately there's a group of thought that babies and young children should never be allowed to invade an aircraft because they'd disturb other passengers with their 'crying and bad behaviour'. So much so that as a parent you could perhaps want to do everything possible to prevent a scenario of attracting the ire of these other passengers. I don't know how legal it is, but realistically some concerned parents have resorted to calming their offspring with medication. If you do decide to go this route, please ask for advice from a medical professional first. And please only resort to giving medication when absolutely vital and not as an 'in case' situation.

When I was travelling with my babies, I got a prescription from my doctor for Phenergan with instructions not to give too much or too little, 'because that could make them livelier'. Needless to say, I never used it but felt some reassurance that if my babies became really upset I had something to hand. I must admit, this was mainly so as not to disturb other passengers such is the feeling that I needed to protect my babies and myself from condemnation, and of course to try to make the flight more comfortable for my babies.

Again, I make mention of Rescue Remedy http://www.bachflower4kids.com/

Parental PR

One idea that a friend of mine had was to fill strip-lock plastic bags with earplugs, sweets, and a hand written card with the words 'I will do everything in my power to make sure my baby doesn't disturb you, but if by any chance she starts to cry, please use the earplugs with my apologies.' Works a treat every time apparently.

Child Safety Restraint System - CRS

The FAA – Federal Aviation Administration advises you to keep your child safe using a CRS – a hard backed chair with restraints with government approval and should have the printed notice, "This restraint is certified for use in motor vehicles and aircraft". Failure to have that notice may mean the chair will be checked in as baggage and go into the 'hold'. Taking this chair could also be useful if you intend hiring/driving a car at your destination. Please do check with your airline re the use of your certified chair.

Or you may wish to invest in the Child Aviation Restraint System – the CARES Flight Harness - to keep your child supersafe and comfortable. Its the only child flight safety harness certified by the Federal Aviation Administration (FAA) and Civil Aviation Authority (CAA) and adapted to fit on a regular plane seat. Suppliers and information on Google.

General information

As with many matters re flying, if you have response emails to your queries, I advise you to print them out and take them with you. So much easier to produce them if you are being queried on an information point rather than rely on words.

More useful information can be found on http://www.faa.gov/passengers/fly_children/

Please don't let others make you feel anxious or inadequate because they don't want a baby or young child on-board with them. Although I've found that if you show you care for the comfort of others around you and endeavour to keep your offspring quiet and happy, you are generally shown not just appreciation but sometimes support too. Its worth putting in the effort to get on with your fellow passengers so that if you need to go off to the loo (or struggle to store things in the overhead locker whilst holding a babe) and you don't have a partner or friend to look after your children/baby to help – look around for that extra pair of hands.

Another thing to think about? If you board the plane anticipating a consuming fear you may well find it affects your baby/child, thereby creating the scenario of an offspring demanding your attention when all you want to do is zone out. With ragged nerves, patience levels are lowered and could result in both you and your baby/child in tears and creating perhaps more noise than you'd really wish. Lock into your exercises, breathe deeply and if needs must – ask for help from the cabin crew, if only to relieve you for a few minutes to walk down the aisle, go fetch a glass of water, go to the loo and refresh yourself. This is so much better than descending into a despairing mess with an unrelenting vocal baby/child.

ARE AIRLINE PRACTICAL COURSES USEFUL?

As I've already mentioned - I help aerophobics by using a bespoke combination of NLP/Hypno/EFT to break down their pattern of fear by getting to the root cause and demolishing it then building positive patterns to allow them to fly without stress.

Sometimes though, its not enough to do the 'mind stuff'. I have had clients who struggled with complete recovery because they needed to know that planes were mechanically safe, certainly enough to trust and keep them safe, and attending relevant airline courses certainly helps with that.

I do believe that attending my sessions, or similar ones, and/or going through the exercises and advice in this book, together with a practical course on understanding planes will demolish your fears completely or certainly put you well on the road to fly in comfort.

Margaret was a particularly interesting client who came to see me a couple of years ago for anxiety re flying. She is a highly, and I do mean 'highly' intelligent lady, with an equally high powered job. Flying was part of the parcel and although she'd been fine with flying for years, suddenly she wasn't. It began with a niggly feeling in the pit of her stomach, and grew into a full-blown fear. Being a strong, determined lady she found this really hard to deal with, and of course, once the attachments were added to the mix – flying turned from a previously innocuous vehicle to get from A to B, to a real fear. I know that her sessions with me helped, but she still needed actual confirmation that the mechanics of a plane were safe, and so she attended a practical course hosted by EasyJet.

I emailed Margaret asking her if she'd share her experience of the Easyjet course with you.

A recommendation from a former client

My email to her:

> *Margaret - I've been working with clients with their flying anxiety and compiling information from research, including which airlines offer re fear of flying courses et cetera, as I've come to the conclusion that a combination of*

what I do together with a flight course gives the best results.

This is all coming together in a self-help book I'm in the process of writing, and I'd love your input as in - was it the Ryanair course you took? And how effective was it? Was there anything you would add to the course to make it better - or anything you can add to the ethos that these courses are worth taking (I believe they are but your thoughts would be much appreciated).

Her answer which puts the case for sessions and airline practical courses so brilliantly:-

"I agree for me it worked well having the combination of the sessions with you and then the course.

I think the sessions helped me to get to a place where I was receptive to the course.

I did the Easyjet one which was over 2 days - and excellent. It was a small lecture theatre style session on the first day for about 4hrs. This covered the way your brain sees what it expects to see/hear and can get into bad thinking patterns which are not based on reality- they explained how to break out of these patterns.

The actual science of flying - with a very sensible mature pilot talking us through why flying is safe.

Techniques you can use to keep calm - you would recognise these.

On the next day the whole group took a flight on a specially chartered flight - quite strange getting on a flight at Manchester airport which was on the board as going to Manchester - confused the passengers on other flights.

It was an hour flight and the leader of the previous days course and the pilot who spoke to us were both in the cabin with us (another pilot was flying the plane), the cabin pilot was miked up and gave a running commentary of what was happening/about to happen/ the noises etc. Most people took a friend with them - Mike came with me - useful as he heard the messages and explanations which he can now repeat to me if I get panicky.

So yes I would recommend the Easyjet course but for me the combination of the sessions followed by the course seems to have been the best. I would also add that as its about breaking patterns of thinking I think you need to fly soon after doing the course and then fly as often as you can - seeing each trip as a step forward and a chance to improve until you really have changed the pattern of your thinking.

I hope this helps? M Edwards, 10th May 2016, England UK

Remember - Airline companies are so aware of passenger anxiety that many offer 'fear of flying' courses to help passengers and potential passengers to at least manage their fears if not get rid of them completely. And ask yourself – would they provide this service if there was no demand for it? Would they offer it if only a handful of people had need of it? The answer to both questions is 'no.' So take heart that you are not alone with your anxiety and practical courses have been developed purely to help you overcome your fear.

YouTube has clips on fear of flying courses too and well worth your time looking for them if you can't attend an actual course.

FLYING *IS* SAFE – SO ARE YOU.

Limited beliefs are the creation of limited knowledge. Limited knowledge harbours fear and uncertainty – become informed and open your mind to new exciting experiences.

There are literally – around the world - hundreds of thousands of ground and flight staff/crew whose whole intention and job is to keep your plane safe – therefore keep *you* safe. Many have specialised training to perform this safety not just adequately but way beyond normal safety margins.

Ever since the first successful passenger-carrying planes were built – safety has been a major aim. Not just to ensure that the pilots, passengers and crew were kept safe, but also to protect the massive investments made to develop, build and fly that aircraft in the first place.

For an example of investment made, as at July 2015 there were 571 Boeing 747s in service and flown by major companies such as British Airways, Cathay Pacific, and Lufthansa. The first 747-100 from the Boeing Company was put into service in 1970. Those first planes sold at a list price of US$24,000,000. That same aircraft if it were to sell today would cost US$146,600,000.

The air industry is worth *Billions* of £s Sterling. You think that that income wouldn't be so protected as to continue to be able to stay in business? Especially when it's such a highly competitive industry.

And the major focus in the protection and safety aspect is – you. Yes, you. Without you and the millions of other passengers carried each year there is no industry. It's that simple. That has to be protected as a priority and at all costs. It is a never-ending programme for companies who build and equip aircraft to not just maintain existing safety features, but improve and expand on them - constantly. Even throughout flights, equipment is being monitored with information being fed back to the requisite departments and areas of expertise on the ground as well as the air.

The Airline Industry as a whole is progressive in the practices of adapting, tightening, and improving passenger/aircraft safety and security to meet and anticipate any possible or perceived threats made to it. And since it's a very competitive market – airlines have to offer you every safety and security practice/feature possible in order for you to even think about flying with them.

(To demonstrate this continuous determination for safety, as at September 2016 many airlines banned the Samsung Galaxy Note 7 mobile phone from flights, although there appears to have been only one incident caused by a Galaxy Note 2 phone. Passengers noticed a burning smell and alerted cabin crew who immediately dealt with it by extinguishing it and putting it in a fire safe container. Samsung's response was to immediately recall this smart phone and in some instances, I believe Samsung set up booths in airports where the 7s could be swapped for safer phones, including transferring data to new phone – good damage control. You may note that advice given out by airlines is that if by chance you should 'lose' your smart phone on the flight, to alert cabin crew who will look for it – which is on board procedure.)

The flight crew, particularly of the more reputable airlines adhere to the strict rules and regulations laid down by the General Civil Aviation Authority (GCAA) and are constantly monitored to ensure that all requirements are being taken.

There is also a Safety Management System (SMS) which is designed to track, report, and manage safety related cases. The GCAA check and audit airline's SMS to ensure the highest International safety standards are maintained.

All this information should alleviate any fear or doubt in your mind. Also be aware that if a sufficient number of passengers become dissatisfied with their experience with a particular airline, the chances are that that airline will be punished by not being the preferred carrier. The results would be a drop in their profits, and in some cases, have sent companies bankrupt due to their poor service.

You may be put off flying for various reasons, but safety and security must not figure in your mind as being a 'cause' of your fear. And if it is – please work to demolish it because it really doesn't merit your worry.

The industry is in a constant growth pattern. More and more people are making more and frequent trips by air – surely that must tell you something too?

To give you some idea of the massive size of the airline industry, consider this report put out IATA:

> *"The International Air Transport Association (IATA) announced an upward revision of its 2015 industry outlook to a $29.3 billion net profit. On expected revenues of $727 billion, the industry would achieve a 4.0% net profit margin. The significant strengthening from the $16.4 billion net profit in 2014 (re-stated from $19.9 billion) reflects the net impact of several global factors, including stronger global economic prospects, record load factors, lower fuel prices, and a major appreciation of the US dollar."*

For your information - *IATA* - the *International Air Transport Association* – works with its airline members and the air transport industry as a whole to promote safe, reliable, secure and economical air travel for the benefit of the world's consumers. *IATA's* 260 member airlines comprise 83% of all air traffic.

IATA's website offers you a wealth of information too, so check it out – www.iata.org

I acknowledge I can have help to release my fear and will ask for it.

THE AIRLINE INDUSTRY, YOU, YOUR COMFORT AND SAFETY.

Once you have enquired about or booked a flight, applied for a passport or a visa or even logged on to a travel site on the internet, various information gathering agencies may collect data about you to create a 'profile' of you for the benefit of your carrier. The airlines have policies in place not to divulge any information about you to any unauthorised businesses and secure your information to prevent this from happening. They use this information not just to ensure that you are safe for them to carry, but also to give them the information to make your flight as comfortable and pleasant as possible, because – as I said before – this is a highly competitive industry. Your airline wants to keep you, not risk sending you off to a competitor.

Profiles are also used by intelligence agencies to ensure potential passengers are legitimate, law-abiding people who are free to fly.

Security Checks

'Security checks' are also made on every airport worker from the person who cleans the floors, to service staff in the restaurants, shop assistants, check-in staff, airline personnel, air crews, baggage handlers – in fact – everyone who works in and around the airport. And this is after they've been thoroughly checked out before being offered a job working there. And those security checks don't end there because this work force is constantly checked and rechecked thereafter. This works in your favour because it prevents risky passengers being allowed to board, and the constant reviews of staff security procedures can invariably highlight any new and potential weakness. Certainly you may hear of someone flying under the radar, but these constant and frequent security checks do weed out these people. Of the millions of air industry workers, these people are so rare as to make 'news'. Travelling with the more known, reputable airlines and from highly reputable airports vastly diminish these instances of security breaches. In the never ending quest for safety, biometric information (fingerprints and iris scans) are becoming more common too – proof positive that all is being done to protect you and the industry.

There is so much common knowledge about the security measures taken by authorities but this knowledge is only the tip of the iceberg. Far more and on very many layers and levels – security worldwide is performed 24/7. Unknown because it is vital for all our safety to keep it secret and secure. I did contact a few security/information agencies enquiring about their processes but each declined not surprisingly.

Surveillance for Your Safety

Airports, airport car parks, lounges, restaurants, terminals, departure gates, arrivals – any area in and around airports is under constant surveillance. There are security personnel everywhere, some you wouldn't recognise as being other than airport workers or passengers. Some airlines even employ Sky Marshalls. Sky Marshalls are undercover law enforcement or counter terrorist agents who travel incognito on board commercial flights to counter/prevent/

contain the now very rare aircraft hijackings, or disruptive passengers.

Police Forces

There are Police personnel throughout airports to keep the peace and deal with anyone who refuses to do so.

Heathrow in London have a permanent Police unit from the Metropolitan Police Service Operational Command Unit (OCU) known as Aviation Security. As do many other airports around the world.

And if that isn't enough to make you feel secure, here's another bit of knowledge to make you feel safe. It's an initiative called the Heathrow Airport Watch and was set up by Aviation Security in 2008. Extract taken from Metropolitan Police Total Policing website:

http://content.met.police.uk/Article/Heathrow-Airport-Watch/1400023607843/1400023607843

Heathrow Airport Watch encompasses both Heathrow and London City airports and recognises the useful roles that aviation enthusiasts/plane watchers have to play in helping to keep both airports safe and they are much valued members of the airport community.

"The scheme provides members with a specially designed identity card, lanyard and card holder which should be worn at all times whilst enthusiasts are engaged in their hobby at Heathrow and London City Airports. It allows genuine enthusiasts to be easily identified by police and security teams at each airport.

Regular visitors to Heathrow and London City are most likely to notice something out of the ordinary on or around the airport. It is hoped that the initiative will encourage enthusiasts to contact us if they do see anything suspicious, whilst allowing us to identify those who are genuinely enjoying their pastime at the airport.

All members will be security checked prior to receiving their card. The scheme is aimed at those who regularly visit Heathrow and London City Airports, but all enthusiasts are welcome to apply. The identity cards cost a one off charge of £7.50 to cover the cost of production and postage.

Since launch the scheme has attracted over 500 applications. There is no limit to the number of members for the scheme – the more eyes and ears the better."

Note – These people are extremely and thoroughly checked out and vetted before any such permission is given to become a member.

Sniffer dogs

Over the past few years and with the advent of terror threats and drug trafficking, airport security has been further tightened, with more advance security operations put into place. As a result, one further sign of security procedures implemented is the introduction of 'sniffer dogs' and their equally highly trained handlers. These units patrol both public and restricted areas of the airport. Their job is to 'sniff' out hazardous items and materials, firearms, drugs, suspicious packages or luggage et cetera and prevent them

Air Rage

With cheaper flights and more airports being built, air travel has opened up the world to millions of aircraft passengers. Staycations and stay at home stag and hen parties are often set aside for the more exotic and exciting overseas holidays and parties. Unfortunately 'air rage' has become more common I'm sorry to say. However, air crew are given rigorous training to contain any such bad behaviour on flights. Airline staff are more vigilant in spotting possible trouble these days and either prevent the boarding of these people, or in one case when I was travelling Ryanair to Spain a group of obviously drunken argumentative passengers were hauled off the plane before it left the gate – much to the relief of the rest of us.

Alcohol and Flying

Having a glass of wine, beer or spirits when you are waiting for your flight in the departure lounge can be pleasant; and sometimes a just reward for overcoming all the hassles that travelling by air entails, but try to stick to the one, or abstain altogether until you get on the flight. Yes, it may sooth ragged nerves but so can your preflight exercises which won't get you into trouble, they're cheaper and won't leave you with a hangover. You won't get so dehydrated either.

I do think a lot of cases of unruly behaviour is due to passengers with a fear of flying, who think alcohol and behaviour influencing drugs will help them to get on the plane and make the flight easier to handle. Admittedly any sympathy for these people goes out the window when they cause problems so they don't really do themselves any favours. I believe there is a movement to stop alcohol being sold and consumed in airport departure lounges and on board to limit the chances of passengers becoming inebriated.

Consequences of drunken behaviour on flights may, in extreme cases - result in planes being diverted to offload these passengers. This course of action creates its own set of problems with airlines losing its landing slot at the scheduled destination and having to queue to land which means late arrival times, transfers missed, and sometimes cancelled altogether. On these, thankfully rare occasions, your airline may have to make alternate arrangements for your onward journey because airline safety regulations regarding flight crew not working over the allotted safety time may prevent your flight continuing.

Aviation Law actually forbids anyone being drunk on a plane and although the practice of this law has not been widely enforced, airlines are preparing to enforce it more often now by denying boarding to anyone intoxicated. Airlines don't however have any control over passengers drinking prior to boarding.

Please don't mix medication with alcohol! I know! For some of you this is not good news, but for your own good – please resist.

Near misses

When you read or hear about planes in a 'near miss' scenario, please know individual aircraft flying space has been calculated with a generous safety margin. Should any plane 'stray' into another's airspace, warnings will go off to alert everyone involved to rectify this situation.

In the very rare event of planes flying within the safety margins of each other, the aircraft itself sets off an alarm to alert the pilots that airspace has been compromised, and action can and will be taken to avoid any possible safety issues.

Stacking

You've counted down the time to touch-down only to find your plane is still in the air with no discernible descent and a feeling that you're going around in circles. Well, you probably are... going round in circles, I mean. This is called 'stacking'. For some reason Air Traffic Controllers have your pilot and plane in a queue. This is usually due to another flight arriving or landing later than their due time, or perhaps because your plane has arrived too late to take up its scheduled 'slot' for landing and has to wait to be given another slot. Any of these reasons can delay the whole estimated time of landings for not just your plane but others too. You may see other planes flying around, rest assured they are complying with safety distances and at no time are these distances compromised.

Each airport has an area to 'stack' planes which is sufficiently far away from the destination airport so as not to interfere with other planes landing and taking off, yet close enough to be able to take up the landing position when directed by ATC

Stacking is just another facet of flying. Its annoying but it happens. Imagine a massive spiral in the sky, planes on all levels flying in the one direction at regulated, safe distances and speeds, and in turn descending when given the directive that its safe to do so and until its time to put the wheels on the ground and taxi you to your gate and disembarkation.

Detouring

Unfortunately these days there are some areas of the world where there is political unrest. If entirely possible airlines will detour around these countries such is their attention to keeping their aircraft, staff and you – safe. A detour or rerouting may add a little time to your flight, but surely it's a small price to pay for your safety and confidence in the airline you've chosen to fly with?

Finally – when things may not go according to plan

Yes, there are the rare occasions when things don't go to plan. Know though your airline company does take extreme measures to keep you safe. From returning to the departure airport or detouring your flight to disembarking unruly passengers, sick people, technology/flight issues, unpredicted weather conditions, whatever may jeopardise the efficient functioning of the plane for the safety of passengers and crew – they will take those measures. Should any such incident take place on your flight, know you are in capable, safe, and practiced hands. Leave it all in their hands and use yours to go through your calming exercises.

Even the most petite and graceful female flight attendant is trained to keep you and her other passengers safe. So next time you fly – and you will – just look at your air crew and have a bit more respect for them and their duties. It's not all about serving coffee, cake and sickbeds.

FACTS ABOUT YOUR FLIGHT CREW

Cockpit Crew

- The Captain is the highest ranking officer on-board and has ultimate responsibility for the aircraft, all other crew, and passengers. He is the chief decision maker.

- The First Officer (co-pilot) is second in command, has the same training as the Captain, and is capable of taking over the responsibility of the aircraft, crew, and passengers if necessary.

- Long haul flights can have Second and Third Officers on-board. Their positions are as relief pilots for the Captain and First Officer to give them a break during the long hours of flying.

- The Cabin Crew are headed up by the Purser who is the senior flight attendant and responsible for his/her cabin crew and passengers. The requirement is to have at least one Cabin Crew for every 50 passengers.

People who choose to make their career ferrying people around the skies don't have to simply have a high intelligence to pass the very many exams and courses necessary for qualification. They also need excellent health and money.

For Pilots, without a Class 1 Medical Certificate and around about £100,000 for approximately 2 years training to get their Airline Transport Pilot Licence (ATPL in the UK and ATP in the States), they wouldn't even get off the ground. So those parameters sieve out quite a few applicants. The financial outlay to learn to become a pilot demonstrates their passion for the job and determination to pass in order not to waste that huge outlay. And, no, that does not mean most pilots are wealthy. Many enter into repayment schemes or manage to obtain loans from the airlines they wish to join, paying off the loan once qualified and employed by said airline.

Qualifications are only obtained once a trainee has passed the required 'modules' through approved flying schools. Flight training initially on light aircraft follows with extra hours in a flight simulator and very intense ground based study.

Eventually and at the end of this training, the pilot will then get their essential multi-engine 'rating'. This allows them to apply for their Commercial Pilot Licence (CPL), it still doesn't allow them to fly airliners, but does allow them to fly business jets. In order to acquire their ATPL there's a whole lot more study, exams to pass, on flight and ground study, AND also build up 'flying hours' of 1,500 hours before becoming a Captain of a plane. Flight training takes anywhere from 4 to 15 years, and participants must be at least 21 years of age. The training period and study is so stringent that it is a self-elimination process with failing trainees just not making the grade. That's just a short summary to give you the assurance that the Captain of your flight is not going to risk doing anything to lose his/her pilots licence.

As a passenger please don't think you can control the aircraft better than the pilot/s – so please don't try to fly the plane for them, you're not qualified enough and you'd scare the pants off any other passenger. Release your need to control over to those who know best, and instead concentrate on controlling your imagination.

I need to focus within.

To help you to gain more specialised information regarding pilots/planes, Patrick Smith has kindly agreed to me recommending him and welcomes enquiries. He is an airline pilot and the host of www.askthepilot.com an excellent website to refer to. He lives in Somerville, Massachusetts, USA and keen to dispel any qualms people may feel about flying. He is the author of 'Cockpit Confidential' and well worth checking out for more in-depth information.

Have faith in the pilots flying your plane. They've had extensive and intensive training. All you have to do is sit back and enjoy, relax in the knowledge they *do* know what they're doing.

Cabin Crew

You may think your cabin crew/attendants are there to serve you food and drinks, ensure your seatbelt is fastened and generally make your flight as pleasant and comfortable as possible. Better revise your thinking because their main job is ensuring you are safe. To storing your luggage properly, prepare first aid kits, demonstrate all safety features – remember these latter duties are not for your entertainment but for your safety. They are in charge of and follow very stringent safety protocols and they are responsible for the efficient application and adherence to them. They have to be fit, not just to serve you your beverages, but in case anyone becomes a bit unruly – they have the training and skills to use verbal negotiation to quieten the passenger down; to the extreme and rarely needed skills of overpowering said person so he/she doesn't disturb any of the other passengers on their plane. They are trained to look out for potentially noisy passengers as well as having the skills to take control if things escalate. Again – that's just a short summary of your cabin crew.

Incidentally, if watching cabin crew go through their safety programme speeds your brain up to think negative thoughts – how about mentally adding a tune to their hand movements. Make it a happy, light-hearted tune though, but do please pay attention to the safety programme, even if you are a seasoned traveller. This knowledge, even if you've seen it so many times before, works in your favour in that your unconscious mind can lock it in, thereby giving you a quiet confidence that you are indeed safe.

A Misconception of a Cabin crew's behaviour

Wonder at the behaviour of cabin staff? I had a client who told me they always looked at the cabin crew to make sure they weren't worried about anything that she then should worry about. She'd think, perhaps they know something I don't; perhaps they don't want to alert passengers, perhaps it's something to do with the flight being delayed? No information given and definitely worried about that. And so her anxiety levels ramped up and she'd be really anxious and the plane hadn't even taken off yet. She watched the doors being closed though. And knew the plane would be moving soon. She'd crane her neck for sight of that crew member who looked worried.

I spoke about this anxious behaviour to a young friend who's cabin crew for a well-known international airline company and she gave me this........

How about another and more likely scenario? The plane was an hour late taking off. To flight crew who have had to arrive at least two hours prior to the flight boarding, the delay has added another hour to their time 'on duty', except – cabin crew don't get paid until the doors shut on the plane. So that makes 3 hours of work with no pay. Plus they have to work faster to prepare the plane for take-off when a slot became free and think about how the impact of added hours makes to their personal itinerary. Now look at that person again. Do they really look like they're bothered by a fantasy scenario of imminent danger, or they were struggling with a payment issue or other innocuous situation?

Do you see how things can escalate in your mind?

I release my need to control to those who are qualified to have control.

PLANES AND THE FLYING INDUSTRY – facts, stats, and info

If your mind is full of flying thoughts, fill it with facts not improbabilities.

Smelly, dangerous, ugly, frightening.........they'll never take on. They're just a fleeting fad.

These were the beliefs of ordinary people when cars were first introduced. The commonly referred to 'horseless carriages' were considered to be such a danger that a 'Red Flag' Law in the United Kingdom was created for the safety of pedestrians and animals. It was a policy that required 'self-propelled vehicles' to be led by a man waving a red flag or lantern to warn of the vehicle's approach.

In America, a 'Red Flag' Law was passed in Vermont in 1894. In Pennsylvania, the Red Flag Law was enacted when legislators were unanimous in supporting and passing a Bill requiring all motorists of "horseless carriages" to take the following action if they chanced upon cattle or other livestock. They had to:

1. Immediately stop the vehicle

2. Immediately and as quickly as possible ... disassemble the automobile

3. Conceal the various components out of sight, behind nearby bushes until equestrian or livestock is sufficiently pacified.

Thankfully for Pennsylvanian motorists the Bill did not become law, because their Governor of the time vetoed it. It still goes to show though how the early cars were perceived so negatively – and with fear.

For your interest, here's a pertinent extract from The Detroit News re motor cars –

Serious debate was held in courtrooms and in editorials over whether the automobile was inherently evil. The state of Georgia's Court of Appeals wrote: *"Automobiles are to be classed with ferocious animals and ... the law relating to the duty of owners of such animals is to be applied. However, they are not to be classed with bad dogs, vicious bulls, evil disposed mules, and the like."* http://www.detroitnews.com

"The horse is here to stay, but the automobile is only a novelty—a fad." This was the advice from a president of the Michigan Savings Bank to Henry Ford's lawyer Horace Rackham. Rackham ignored the advice and invested $5000 in Ford stock, selling it later for $12.5 million.

'Dangerous, frightening, a fad'………. Virtually the same words spoken about aeroplanes. Can you see the pattern developing here? New, extraordinary inventions were, and still are, viewed with distrust and suspicion.

As it turns out – the introduction of the smelly dangerous motor car was much safer than unpredictable horses, and the introduction of planes is a much safer way of getting over distances than cars.

Everything is relative but worth consideration.

As far back as historic records and reports began – humans have looked up at the sky, and watched birds flap their wings or glide on thermals with an envious freedom of being able to go wherever they wanted – and those humans dreamt of owning that freedom of flight for themselves. To lift them up to an experience of immeasurable pleasure and adventure. To fly to places never before visited, to take them out of their perpetually grounded lives – to have freedom.

YOU have that choice, you have that freedom to transport yourself through the sky to other places, other adventures, other experiences – why not do it with pleasure?

Planes were built for our enjoyment and ease of taking us to places that most people would never have even known existed before. They're comfortable, beautiful and highly sophisticated in their design and engineering.

From those historic aspirations and desire to fly, men began to make contraptions in order to lift them up into the sky – to fly and glide like an eagle. Unfortunately these earlier attempts usually ended up like a stoned crow grounded in a dishevelled mess. Progress since then has been profound.

Some facts:

- Planes have flown commercially since the 1st of January 1914 (the St. Petersburg-Tampa Airboat Line in the USA).

- There are currently over 5000 IATA coded airlines operating around the world.

- In 2015 – nearly 3.6 BILLION (3,600,000,000) passengers flew in commercial airplanes.

- Formulated statics show that there are approximately 650,000 people in the air right now.

- The odds of being in a plane crash is so slim it's hard to quantify in real terms, but its put at something so remote as 1:11,000,000 – and that doesn't necessarily mean resulting in injury or death.

- The odds of a fatal car crash are put at 1:5000.

If the above fact disturbed you please tap it out or resolve it immediately in your mind - that you are not and never will be in that airline statistic.

- Before an aircraft can be given certification to carry passengers, new planes are put through rigorous tests and many flying hours by test pilots.

- Emergency situations are tried, tested and practiced (on a regular basis) by all air crew to ensure efficiency, and that safety regulations are met. For instance, in the event of the deployment of the 'escape slide' (when the plane is on the ground and quick evacuation of the plane is necessary), cabin crew are trained to perform this operation with efficiency and speed. They are also highly trained to take charge and direct passengers in the rare event of a landing on water. Trust them.

For your interest and education, Thomas Noack of Plane Spotters has kindly given me permission to give you their website

www.planespotters.net

they provide information on aircraft, for example:

- 127,170 Registrations
- 39,573 Airframes

- 5,476 Airlines

And host a total of:

- 549,806 Aviation Photos
- 401,476 High-Quality Aviation Photos of aircraft

I know I am safe to fly.

Facts about aircraft and how they're constructed

All planes have an engine. Whether it's a jet engine producing 'thrust' or a propeller plane which needs an engine to turn the propeller.

Before a plane is built, the design process begins with thousands of man hours of specialised engineering designing, discussing, testing, problem-solving, drawings made, adapted, redrafted and so on. Then they are submitted to the many levels of national aviation airworthiness authorities before the design can be passed for 'test' construction.

The prime aim in design of an aircraft is safety, and to pass the very stringent aircraft construction regulations and laws, which again – have been made with your safety and the safety of the aircraft paramount.

The construction of an aircraft then takes place with every bolt, screw, material, fabric, technology used et cetera having to go through very rigorous testings and retestings. Each step is overseen by specialised inspectors all looking for fault. Not only is the aircraft built for safety, it is built to survive crashes.

Planes are put through the most rigorously extreme tests, and stress tests – way beyond what it would go through even in the most appalling conditions. For instance, re turbulence – the uncomfortable bane of even the most seasoned passenger – the plane is tested in a specially designed wind tunnel and put through winds that are so chaotic and massive they don't even exist in real life. Other safety features are all designed and built with equally massive safety margins – way beyond what is needed for safe, efficient flying. And the design process never ends, always looking at ways to improve.

You may be interested to know that there are 'Let's Visit Airbus' tours. If you'd like to see the final assembly of the A320 to A380 you may visit them in Hamburg Finkenwerder, and for a reasonable admission price – you will be shown, informed and questions answered during this 2hr 30min programme. There is a site in Bremen where you will see their specialised wing production and a site in Stade specialising in carbon fibre components. Airbus has a tour in Toulouse too – where the main feature is to go behind the scenes and witness a test flight.

And no! Wings do not fall off during flights. Aircraft wings are specifically designed to deal with any weather pattern. Yes, they move, yes they 'bounce' as one client put it, but that is what they are designed to do. They don't just hang there rigidly on either side of the plane, they are a magnificent piece of sophisticated engineering. Obviously vital to flying, but did you know that they also help to limit the effects of turbulence?

How do planes lift, fly and land?

A common myth around modern aerodynamics and our understanding of flight stated "according to modern aerodynamics the bumblebee shouldn't be able to fly, but the bumblebee doesn't know this, so it flies anyway." Scientists have, time and again, proven this to be factually incorrect. The method of how the humble bumblebee produces sufficient lift to propel its corpulent body skyward is well understood by modern aerodynamics. What's the point of this? The point is there are many myths and outdated data about 'flight' that simply do not hold true when put against the modern understanding.

The simplest understanding of how planes fly is as follows:-

Airflow over a rounded wing will produce an area of low pressure on the top of the wing. The pressure being lower on the top of the wing quite literally propels the aircraft skyward. To get a more complete understanding we are going to have to get a little bit into the maths behind 'lift'. The amount of lift produced by a wing dynamic is governed by the lift equation:

$L = \tfrac{1}{2} \rho V^2 C_L S$

Where:

L = Lift Produced

ρ = Air Density

V = Velocity

C_L = Co-efficient of lift (Attained from the Angle of Attack and shape of the wing)

S = Surface Area of the Wing

What does this all mean to you? Not a whole lot really, but what it means to a pilot is there are three vital parts he can control.

Velocity ie forward speed

Coefficient of lift

Surface area of the wings

Velocity. Jet engines work by taking a small mass of air and shooting it backwards at a high speed, the resulting force propels the plane forward. This is all in accordance with Newton's 3rd law of motion. "For every reaction there is an equal and opposite reaction." The pilot can alter the size of this reaction i.e. how much thrust he wants by changing the quantity of fuel added to the *engines which in turn, changes the level of jet thrust.*

Co-efficient of lift. This is slightly more difficult to explain but it simply boils down to the angle at which the aerofoil hits the airflow which determines the co-efficient of lift along with the wing shape. You can't change the wing shape but you can change the way the wing hits the airflow. You can experiment with this in your car on the highway. When you hold your hand out flat you shouldn't feel much force pushing your hand either way but when you rotate your hand so that the front part is higher than the back you feel your hand want to travel skywards. This is actually you changing the co-efficient of lift of your hand. This is exactly the same principal on how planes climb and take-off. The pilot pulls back on the control which causes the nose to rise and tail to drop and changes the way the wing hits the airflow, causing the plane, just like your hand, to fly upwards.

Surface area. Have you ever wondered why, when coming in for a landing you see the flaps extending out from the wing? This is the pilot actually altering the size of the wing. Why does he do this? When a plane needs to land it doesn't want to be going as fast as it was flying at high level. There's only a certain amount of runway available and certain amount the tyres can take. Hence, he uses the flaps to increase the amount of lift produced by the wing and therefore reduces his velocity for landing, ensuring you touchdown at a reasonable speed and safely.

There have been very many years of engineering research gone into the designing of aircraft, to be more efficient and safe. Each existing plane in service today was – and still is - rigorously tested, including being battered in wind tunnels to evaluate the strength and flexibility of the wings of a plane for any and all weather conditions. 75,000 hand drawings were made by the engineers of the original prototype of the 747 (Jumbo Jet) before it was built for service.

In summary, the crux of how planes fly is well known and has been significantly improved over the years, particularly with the advent of computer modelling. When flying in an aircraft you can be sure that all the fundamentals of

Newton's laws are in force and it's simply our superior knowledge of the forces at play and our ability to exploit them to our needs that gives birth the miracle that is safe, powered flight.

Information thanks to FLT LT Michael Hannan, RAAF 2016

Flying in general and your safety

Long before you even step into an airport, teams of specialised workers and staff have been checking, repairing, providing maintenance, rechecking (again and again) every feature of your plane to unsure your safety to the highest degree. Systematic duties performed by both manual workers and highly sophisticated technology.

And it doesn't stop once you are in the air. There is a continual process, with monitoring of the plane's computers and structure as it is in the air with information fed back to base computers, not just for the airline/airline manufacturer to ensure the safety and efficiency of said aircraft, but there are multi-layers of safety regulations to adhere to too with very stiff penalties for non-observance.

Top concern from passengers who have a fear of flying is - Turbulence.

Planes do sometimes go through turbulence, that's a fact. However, if you are well-prepared and expect turbulence on your flight, it will only be a mild discomfort or inconvenience, not a reason to think you are in any danger.

You may have been given the advice that 'a plane experiencing turbulence is like driving on a bumpy road'. It's a good analogy but probably not the greatest comparison. And if you don't know the facts and safety features of planes whilst experiencing turbulence – you'd probably wish to be in that car, on the ground – even if it is 'bumpy'.

Turbulence is nothing new; we experience 'turbulence' in various areas of our lives. It's how *you* deal with that turbulence that creates the 'blue-print' in your unconscious mind.

First and foremost it is important to be aware that turbulence is a fact of flying and nothing to be feared. The airline's flight planners will have already taken into consideration any possible weather pattern that may produce turbulence and will reroute the plane around it wherever possible. In the air, pilots will avoid it if they can, not because they think the plane will be in danger, but so that you the passenger will experience minimal discomfit. Planes are built to deal with it as I previously stated, and to withstand far greater turbulence than they'd ever have to encounter. On the rare occasions that there's been a sudden change in weather pattern, pilots of other planes will inform any plane travelling the same route so that avoidance can be made if necessary.

You have to play your part too. Safety features are there for you to take advantage of whilst going through turbulence, so if the seat belt sign goes on - adhere to it. Please don't think that this is the best opportunity to visit the loo because there won't be a queue, and yes, some people do do that! Injuries happen more to passengers and crew who are not wearing their seat belt whilst going through these 'bumps'. 'Turbulence' can take the form of a light movement that barely disturbs the surface of your water/coffee/tea cup on your tray, to the less frequent – hold on to your cup so it doesn't spill over. In fact, some people who test this with a cup of liquid on their table get relief from seeing how little the surface is disturbed. Try it next time and have fun with it.

And always remember – you have stress-less exercises to go through, use them, that's what you have them for.

Depending on the level of your anxiety, perhaps don't fly when there is a greater chance of severe turbulence, ie during monsoon seasons, till at least you have your anxiety either under control or demolished completely. It's better to have positive flights to build on. Sometimes, the little turbulence you feel may be the ripples from a more unsettled weather pattern and the pilot is taking his plane around it instead of flying through it. The thought to always keep in mind is that, if you do experience a bumpy flight, you will still be safe, the plane will not break up, and the pilot has the technology to avoid it, detour around it or deal with it with immense skill and experience.

From a previous nervous flyer:

"I made it from London to New York with a bit of turbulence. I'd spoken to the flight crew when boarding about how nervous I was and they reassured me I'd be okay. I must have looked sceptical because one of the crew went to get the pilot. I asked him if he was nervous when he flies through storms and he said, 'Never'. He said he'd flown over 10,000 hours and never been concerned. He assured me that there are many layers of back-up systems should something not work to its optimum level, and even more safe guards supporting those. He also said to sit over the wing if possible because it doesn't feel so bumpy there, those seats are the steadiest in the aircraft, and not to sit at the tail end of the plane which can be uncomfortable if there's turbulence. Listening to him speak so confidently made me feel calm and at ease. When there was a bit of turbulence during my flight, I still felt okay. You're right Linda, knowledge is power.

I'd advise any nervous flyer that If they get the chance ask to speak to the flight crew, especially the pilot/captain, take it and hopefully he/she will come and speak to you to make you more at ease."

Can doors be opened in flight?

The quick answer is – no! Aircraft doors CANNOT be opened in flight for the simple reason that the difference in air pressure between the inside and outside of the plane will not allow it. Patrick Smith from Ask the Pilot explains the technicalities of this on his website – www.askthepilot.com

Next time you board a plane, take a good look at the door and frame you are going through. Notice how it almost replicates a vacuum flask, in that the door acts as a 'plug' which, when closed, secured and in the air 'seals' the door to the aircraft body.

Can windows open during flight?

As with aircraft doors, the simple answer is no, due to their design and to the pressure involved. Neither can they fall out.

What's the little hole in the bottom of the window?

It's a safety feature called a breather hole and it's used to regulate and equalise the amount of pressure that passes between the window's inner and outer panes. (Commercial aircraft usually have 3 panes) It also prevents the fogging up of windows and keeps them clear. Don't be in the least concerned if there is a little bit of moisture present on the inner pane, its purely due to condensation as you would find on your windows at home.

Why do window blinds have to be up during take-off and landing?

It's a precautionary CAA Regulation to ensure window blinds are up for take-offs and landings, because in the event of an emergency, it allows the Emergency services to look into the plane and assess the situation. Another reason is so that natural light can replace cabin lights should there be an electrical malfunction.

Why are lights in the cabin dimmed?

As a precautionary measure, the lights in your cabin have to be dimmed on landing at night time, so that passenger's eyes are adjusted to the low light in case of emergency evacuation. It also allows passengers to see the emergency floor lights to follow for evacuation.

Why can't I use my phone whilst in the air?

Before take-off you will be asked to switch your phone off or switch to 'Flight Mode'. Not for the reason most people think – ie the phone could interfere with onboard technology and cause serious issues, (so if you see someone on their phone, don't freak out it won't cause the plane to crash). What it could do though is create interference to the pilot's headphones filling them with that buzzing noise you get when you put your phone near a speaker. And who wants a cross pilot?

Be aware that on Qantas, British Airways and Cathay Pacific you may be hear the message that should you lose your phone/iPad on the flight to please ask one of the flight crew to look for it.

This is because it contains a lithium battery and should be kept safe from any damage should it get squashed down your seat. There has been one reported incident of a damaged phone potentially causing a problem but was swiftly dealt with, and the result is this new message to passengers.

Drones or UAVs

Rules, laws, regulations, registrations, and examinations of drones and the flying thereof are being made and enforced by many countries to ensure the complete safety of aircraft. There have been recorded incidents whereby drones have flown close to planes, but there is more chance of that drone being shot out of the sky by some annoyed farmer trying to round up his spooked cows again, than a drone bringing down an aircraft. Certainly drones can interfere with flight plans, communications et cetera and all these areas are under close scrutiny by both airlines, the AFF, the CAA, other regulating bodies around the world, and respective governments to set ever higher standards of safety.

Engine noise

Does the noise made by an engine bother you? I've had people say that the noise of the engines roaring during the run up to take off and when they land has made them anxious – frankly if I didn't hear any noise from the engines I'd be anxious. Think of it this way – in order to have lift off, the engines have to be revved up to create the speed and the propulsion to lift it from the ground – systems normal. And on landing, thrust reversers on the engines are deployed to help slow down the aircraft which in turn means less stress on the brakes. So next time you're on a plane – take great heart and comfort from that roar.

Flight Plans

Long before your plane is readied for your flight – flight plans have already been submitted, scrutinised by the relevant sections, factored into your flight, and rechecked again before being passed. They feature in the pre-flight briefings all pilots and crew have to attend prior to boarding the plane. Flight Plans are legal documents which are filed with the local authority. They cover aspects such as – weather, routes, air safety as in avoiding flying over volatile countries, air traffic et cetera.

Flight delays

Probably too often these days, passengers may experience delays to their flights. I advise checking with the airline you're booked with for any news on delays. Log on to your airline's website and/or Departures information on the relevant airport's website to check. It's better to wait out some of this time at home rather than the airport.

Delays are due to a whole host of reasons and shouldn't be taken for anything other than what they are – delays. Of course, if you intend taking a connecting flight, this may cause you some angst so to limit that, make enquiries, ask your airline to help with this factor. Any reputable airline will do all they can to fix this and lessen your anxiety of missing a connecting flight as much as they can.

Flight delays are more usually caused by weather conditions. If the weather isn't safe to fly, there will be a delay until it is. Either way planes will be grounded, stacked (circling the air) or diverted until the weather is safe for aircraft again. It should be said that planes can fly through practically any weather situation, but the comfort of passengers is paramount and airlines would choose to keep it that way. Fog can be an issue with landing planes, not from a safety point of view but, once on the ground, the process of taxiing to the dock et cetera takes longer than on clear days and that must be factored in.

Other reasons for flight delays are perhaps the plane you are flying out on was delayed arriving. Or there may have been late passengers checking in and clearing security. Rest assured that if your plane is delayed, its due to a very good reason all coming down to your safety and comfort. Delays to departures can and will probably result in your plane losing its 'take-off slot' and will incur a significant financial penalty to the airline concerned. And don't forget, each plane has to go through rigorous security checks before being cleared to take on its passengers and fly. So yes, delays can be annoying, but they are not red flag alerts to be concerned about.

Night flying navigation

Planes have been built to fly at night. They have highly sophisticated flight instruments to carry you through the air safely. These instruments are sensitively designed to give the pilots all the information they need without it having to be 'daylight', so please rest assured – night flying is safe. Pilots use these instruments for every situation, altitude, weather, sticking to the flight path or 'corridor' that has been given to them for every step of the way.

What happens when an Engine Malfunctions?

Another prime concern for anxious passengers is if an engine ceases to work properly. Here are the facts though –

Modern commercial aircraft are designed to fly safely in the rare event that an engine malfunctions because the other engines are perfectly adequate to fly the plane effectively. The aircraft's sophisticated on-board technology together with highly trained pilot skills can adjust to and handle this situation safely. Pilots undergo specific, ongoing and thorough training in this aspect. In the truly extraordinary event of all engines malfunctioning, technology and systems are in place to handle such a rare situation in that the aircraft is designed to glide to the nearest place of landing. An example of which was the Air Transat Flight 236 which experienced a complete engine loss over the Atlantic Ocean in 2001. The aircraft glided 75 miles to a runway on the Azores islands with all passengers and crew landing safely.

Re manmade incidents:

I'm not going to say anything about hijacks and sabotage because the chances of you experiencing any is 1 in 10,408,947 over the past 10 years. And the chances due to constantly upgraded security measures are decreasing every day.

In summary:

Anxious anticipation of something you have never experienced before can generate into an overwhelming feeling that voids any excitement or joy. As with flying – learn as much as you can before you step onto that plane. The internet is full of more information about flights, planes, airports et cetra than ever before.

I'VE NEVER BEEN ABLE TO GET ON A PLANE - *BEFORE.*

I've had people who've said they've been so terrified of planes that they've never flown.

Now, if you take that literally, it doesn't make sense. How can you possibly fear something you've never experienced?

Because its fear by transference. In other words, they have put an experience they've had of being frightened but transferred that fear onto planes and flying. On the face of it, it's an illogical fear, yet it proves that it's the attachments to the original thought/experience that's created a situation whereby the issue has become so overwhelming for them – they'd never even been able to even think of booking a ticket never mind step on a plane.

There have been and still are – many many people who've given up lucrative jobs, missed seeing family, missed seeing the world – simply because of a fear that does not have its basis in actual flight. Can you imagine the feelings they have as a consequence?

So for those people I say, break down that fear into bite sized pieces because it's when we try to see the whole scenario, it becomes too big in our mind, then our body reacts until the very thought produces something akin to panic and no-one enjoys that sensation. Also, each time you go through this scenario, your reaction attaches to the original giving you overwhelm and the belief you simply can't fly.

Turn your future trip into an adventure. Fill your head with knowledge and information. If it's a social flight ie non business, what best deals can you get? What are local customs? List what you'd like to do/see/hear/feel/taste? Even for business trip people – if you had a window of opportunity in your diary – where would you like to spend it? What can you find out that I haven't already covered? – Let me know.

Most of all – ask for support and encouragement, not just from family and friends – find internet forums to comment on, I have one on Facebook – www.facebook.com/groups/160144194333571 please join, accept and give support to other likeminded people.

A case in point:

I had a client who was an executive in a large corporation. He was being offered a highly sought after position within the Group with an envious salary package and perks but he was reluctant to take it up because it required extensive overseas meetings with other executives of this International Group. He believed he didn't have the confidence to lead these people of different cultural backgrounds, customs and language. We worked on this for a couple of sessions and as he grew in confidence about speaking to these different nationalities, he couldn't quite make that final step into full confidence, and this, despite working through his homework to combat his fear completely.

Through further NLP elicitation we discovered it wasn't so much the fear or reticence of speaking at these meetings, but that he was expected to make his presentations to clients and other staff of these overseas operations. There seemingly was the problem. He could deliver everything required of him at his company office here in the

UK, but had trouble when having to make overseas presentations.

Delving yet deeper, it was revealed that although he had this top job here in the UK, he had never been on a plane. If he had to go to Europe, he would drive. If he had to go further afield – he'd organise Conference calls. Anything to avoid being on a plane which brought him out into a sweat just thinking about it. He was so clever with avoiding planes that his employers put it down to the fact that he was 'budget effective' and applauded his dedication.

The proposed new position of course involved extensive air travel. He had thought he'd be able to control his fear with calming drugs and had tried them in anticipation only to realise that he wasn't 'as sharp' (his words) when delivering his presentation the following day. This gave him some angst that he wasn't doing the great job his self-satisfaction and his company demanded. It also eroded his confidence, but when we linked this back to previous experiences – out came his fear of flying.

He hadn't been aware of the root of this fear, but as we unravelled it, his whole physiology changed from being slumped in his chair, to sitting upright and forward – and excited.

Using a combination of hypnosis and NLP, I took him back to when he was 6 years old. He used to make model aeroplanes with his father and loved spending that one to one time with his dad. Each time they finished a plane, his father would hang it from my client's bedroom ceiling with thread so that it appeared to be flying. As a 6 year old, my client was very happy about having a ceiling of planes flying over him.

One night, a model plane fell from the ceiling onto his head whilst he was sleeping. Naturally he awoke with fright. He called out to his parents who came rushing into his room, turning on the lights – and there on his pillow was the small balsa wood plane which had come undone from its thread.

He described to me how he and his parents laughed, then his mother cuddled him and tucked him back up in his bed, and he never thought anything about it. – Until we unearthed the memory.

And that dear readers is where his fear of getting on a plane started. With a fright when he was a small boy. His mother hugging him not only quelled his fright, but also unknowingly anchored the fear into his mind.

He had still enjoyed making model aeroplanes with his father and until the day we elicited where this fear began he didn't realise how this relatively minor incident had created the full blown fear he had as an adult faced with travelling around the world.

I am happy to tell you that, that was his last session with me, although he did email me some months later saying his fear of flying had completely disappeared after that session and he no longer had to resort to avoidance, drugs or alcohol. Could I however, help him to deal with the boredom on long haul flights?

Giving you this case example – can you see how something so minor as a light, tiny toy plane created an overwhelming and almost debilitating fear?

And like my client, once you an unearth that original incident/experience you can see it for what it actually is and find it easier to collapse your fear armed with that knowledge.

*** The more I learn the less I fear.***

MONITORING, GUIDING AND GROUND TO AIR COMMUNICATION

From the moment your plane moves away from the departure gate to when it arrives at the destination's arrival gate it is constantly monitored by a whole team of people and departments – throughout the entire flight.

Air Traffic Control (ATC)

ATC plays a major part in your safety and the safety of your aircraft. At the airport you may see their glass observation rooms on the top of tall towers prominently displayed and in clear sight of the runway/s. They work together with a bigger ATC unit usually sited away from the airport. Their control rooms/buildings are equipped with the most relevant and sophisticated technology and communication as is possible. Air Traffic Controllers control not just the flights going in and out of their specific airport, but also other aircraft flying in the area of between 5 to 10 nautical miles from their jurisdiction.

They are in contact with flight crews, ground crews, and direct the planes onto specified runways – that they've pre-planned. They work to very strict rules, regulations, specific policies and cover many procedures including using radar not just for aircraft but also the weather which is important to safe landings and take-offs. It's a highly specialised, highly responsible job requiring adept minds, quick thinking and problem-solving. ATC also provides services and information to planes en route to and from other airports. As your flight progresses from one area/country, it is in contact with the relevant ground control you're flying over. Information such as weather, conditions, flight paths, and other flights is constantly being fed to the pilot/s and calculations are made to make your flight as smooth, safe and comfortable as possible. The sky is their domain. They work it and guard it rigorously.

NATS (National Air Traffic Services) is the independent British organisation of air traffic controllers/providers who look after the airspace over the United Kingdom. They are sited in a fairly remote area of Hampshire and funnily enough, nowhere near any airport. They use highly sophisticated technology to control the skies over Britain, and their website is worth a look. NATS not only provides air traffic control, they also have a sophisticated Research and Development department which is constantly looking at ways to enhance the safety and efficiency of flying not just for the commercial companies but also military. In other words they have command of the skies over the United Kingdom, and from other sites they control airspace in other countries too.

http://www.nats.aero/

In the United States of America, Air Control Centers work the skies and all the US centres are under the control of National Airspace System which allows for coordination throughout the United States.

RAF – Royal Air Force

Is another body that looks after you and the skies over the United Kingdom.

Any unofficial/unidentified infiltrators of air space and who do not respond to orders from

NATS can find themselves dealing with the highly trained fighter jets/pilots of the Typhoons of the Royal Air Force, whereby the infiltrator will be quickly intercepted, escorted away from UK airspace or face the threat of being brought down, by a manoeuvre of being 'shepherded' to land. If this instruction is ignored, the infiltrator will be given fair warning to remove themselves from the airspace or to be escorted to land. If all else fails and is ignored, the Prime Minister is informed and she/he can give the order to- bring down that aircraft so that it doesn't present any danger.

The RAF have their own Air Traffic Control/lers dotted around the UK and they work in conjunction with NATS and vice versa.

This safety guarding of planes and the skies is not just limited to the UK, other countries also use their Military in the same way.

PREPARE AND PLAN FOR A WORRY FREE TRIP

There is a tendency for aerophobics to avoid anything to do with flying and that includes planning properly for a worry free flight. This can only lead to more stress, therefore more negative attachments being made to flying.

Whereas the actual planning process may act to alleviate worry and work towards giving you a feeling of being in control from the start.

- Make sure, if going overseas that your Passport is current with at least 6 months validity on it. Some countries will not let you enter if you don't comply with their regulation on this.

- Check if you need visas and/or vaccinations

- Organise Travel Insurance from a reputable insurance company, and even then – please read the small print.

- Certainly until you become more confident with flying, please consider using only reputable airlines.

- Do let your airline and/or travel agent know that you are an anxious flyer – most airlines are aware of nervous passengers and will do all they can to allay any discomfort. That also includes flight and cabin crew.

- Check what your airline company expect from you and what they offer, for example – what baggage limit do they set?

- Weigh your baggage before leaving your home, but on scales sitting on a solid floor for accurate results.

- Check your transport and route to the airport, are there any diversions for road works et cetera, does your car have enough petrol?

- If taking public transport, ie a coach – where will it drop you off? A car – where will you be able to park? Do you need to use a valet service?

- Check with your airline what you are allowed to take on board with you so that you are not stopped at security and therefore delayed. For instance, in the UK there are limits to the quantity of liquids you can take on board, and absolutely nothing sharp – even nail scissors are a no-no.

- Check also what the country you are visiting allows you to both bring in and take out.

- I strongly advise investing in a travel pouch to keep all your documents together. I also keep some notes of money in mine in case I need them to hand.

- Check that your Credit Cards et cetera are still valid. If buying your airline ticket online with a third party and with a credit card, make sure you take that credit card with you to the airport as verification. To not do this could cause you problems.

- Do you need Traveller's Cheques?

- Exchange enough money into the local currency of your destination, for emergency spending, porters, taxis et cetera.

- Write down all identification of your Passport, Credit Cards and all other documentation. Photocopies are good. And keep them all in another piece of luggage – just in case they get lost, at least you have details with which to go to consulates, travel agencies, banks et cetera

- Pack spare underwear and perhaps a t-shirt in your cabin baggage in case you need them.

- Do you need to take medication with you? Do you have enough to take?

- Wear as few items of clothing that have metal on them so you don't set off the metal detector going through ground security, which will only delay you.

- Wear comfortable clothes – you may be sitting for a while and being fed more than you would normally eat.

- Pack all your entertainment items in a cabin bag, ie colouring-in books, crayons, headphones, music, ipad, eReader, Kindle, laptops, notebooks, your fly bible/diary, socks, regulation permitting snacks, books, magazines – the latter two being ones you'd really read on board and not ones that you think will improve your intelligence – you want entertainment after all. Oh – and your small stress balls, calming essential oils in bottles of 100mls or 3.4oz, origami sets –

think of all the paper swans you can make to give away to all the passengers and crew around you (only kidding.) Wet wipes and snacks are handy too.

- Re liquids in your cabin baggage – check with your airline just what you are allowed and what falls into the 100mls limit because I believe even gels, lotions and cream as in face-cream are classed in this limit.

- Check before you leave home that your flight is still leaving at the designated time. Delays do occur and you want to know about them to factor them into your timetable rather than spend more time in a departure lounge.

- Check your Passport has the requirements your destination country insist on. For instance, since the 1st of April 2016, travellers to the United States of American were refused entry because their Passports were not biometric or E-passports – passports containing chips with biometric information about the holder.

- Check whether you can buy time/temporary membership in one of the airline's private lounges which gives you access to a whole host of perks, food, beverages – hot/cold, alcoholic/non-alcoholic, comfortable seating, Wi-Fi, sometimes showers too, and so on

Be prepared for delays.

Factor into your time scale, time for delays, for extra security, for long queues both for check-in and security.

If you are delayed, how to spend that time till departure call? Have sufficient cash to purchase snacks and drinks. Many airports these days offer games, massages, showers, Wi-Fi broadband as well as the more usual restaurants, cafes, bars – all may require spending money.

A tip to help you in the event of delays – don't just find a seat to curl up on – walk. As in *stride* like you own the place and with confidence. Not only will you get much needed exercise to counter the time you spent seated on your plane, it'll use up 'time' and will generate endorphins – those delightful, feel good natural chemicals your body produces.

I'm at ease with myself and ready to fly.

A PERSONAL EXPERIENCE OF AN EMERGENCY LANDING

As I've maintained throughout this book, your fear is your own, the air industry is safe, pilots are skilled et cetera, but there are some aerophobics who don't entirely believe that and let their imagination think all sorts of terrible things, so here is a story about an experience a school friend had some years ago. It rather proves my point about having a core experience when probably young and vulnerable which progressed with added attachments to create the fear.

Yes, things - although so very very rarely - can go wrong, and to an aerophobic whose imagination can run riot to feed the fear, for others who don't have any fear or attachments to flying simply don't let any experience affect their love of flying. Its important to replace what your imagination does to you with fact and real life experience.

During the course of my research to write this book I delved deeply into how pilots are so very skilled in any situation, planes more robust, and not least - in order to prove my theory that the initial reason for aerophobia and its attachments that fears stem from something other than planes/flying. I also spoke with people who, even though they had experienced daunting situations, their love and enjoyment of flying remains strong.

I have an old school friend who I reconnected with about a year ago during my research. His name is Iain Webster and his career in life has revolved around the airline industry. He was the most perfect person to ask about flying. I told him I was writing this book and we had a discussion on the possible causes of a person's fear. He vindicated my belief that people feared flying due to an unresolved experience in their lifetime. I asked him that having worked in Emergency Response and all that that entailed (Lockerbie to 9/11), did he have any discomfort in flying. He promptly said, "No! The rewards are greater than the incidents. I enjoy flying so much and the odds of anything life limiting happening are too negligible to think about."

His attitude to flying given his experiences intrigued me, and I asked him if he would write something to put in this book to show you that even when flights don't go according to plan you will still be safe because all the powers that be are focused on you and the aircraft's safety.

Iain has spent several decades in a business career spanning 3 international airlines. Over the years he has been intimately involved in crisis management for incidents ranging from Pan Am 103, Lockerbie to 9/11 and beyond.

He flies frequently for business, now working for a marketing agency that develops and operates airline frequent flyer programmes. On leisure trips Iain and his wife, Linda, favour Asia and Africa as well as visiting their daughter in New York and other family in Texas.

How do you think the odds of being killed in a plane crash compare with the odds of winning the lottery? I could give you the numbers, but there is no point because your emotional attitude to each of these activities will swamp the facts. One you wish with all your might. The other?

All you need to know is that the odds of either happening to you are roughly similar, in the same ballpark. And the chances in both cases are infinitesimal. So there you have it upfront, the good news and the bad news. Reassuring isn't it? Still think you can win the lottery? Don't go there! Stop it now!

If you are a frequent flyer you have probably heard more than once your smug pilot telling you upon landing that the safest part of your journey is now over. He is quite correct. Your odds of being killed in a car accident are literally thousands of times greater. 2,200 times greater if you want to know the number. But you probably don't care about that. We humans don't relate well to statistical odds. We prefer hopes and fears. That's why week after week millions of us buy a lottery ticket hoping that our number will come up. And that's why this book has been written to help conquer the completely illogical fears of those who are convinced their number will be up if they step on a plane.

I have lost count of the number of journeys I have flown both for pleasure and for business. I stopped counting my transatlantic crossings when the number breached 100. And as for the rest of the world, I eventually had to agree with my wife that saving my boarding passes did make me look like a bit of a sad train spotter. I threw them away by the sackful.

Despite all this, and a career spanning several decades in the airline business I have to admit two things. One, I have absolutely no idea how planes fly. Yes I have had the whole high speed low pressure principle explained to me countless times but I still don't get it. It's not natural, is it? Several hundred tons of metal flying through the air carrying 300 people eating chicken. Aren't we clever? Even chickens can't do this. OK, come to think of it, chickens can't actually fly to begin with so forget I said that. And number two, I am definitely not a plane spotter. I can just about distinguish a 747 from a helicopter but that's it.

It's not what planes are, it is what they can do that interests me. Basically they conquer distance in a way no other machine can. They take your body somewhere else faster than your mind can follow. I woke up this morning in London and now I am having dinner in Zambia. That cannot be right. Wow!

I made my first flight when I was 15 years old. For reasons I won't bore you with my pal Allan and I had to fly home from the island of Islay, off the west coast of Scotland to Glasgow at the end of our summer holidays. It was the only way to get back quickly. I remember going into the bank and writing a cheque to cash £15 to pay for the ticket. ATMs had not yet been invented. Expensive for a short flight. We arrived at Islay airport only to be told there would be a short delay while a man in a land rover drove out to clear the sheep off the grass runway. And then the little propeller plane touched down. We boarded and were off within minutes. I don't remember being offered speedy boarding, or seat selection, or a pre-take-off glass of something bubbly. Barely had we taken off than the plane started to descend. Oh my god, was something wrong? No, the pilot announced we would drop down into Campbeltown to pick up some more passengers. Minutes later we were off again and quickly landed in Glasgow. In 20 minutes flying time we had re-traced our outward boat journey that had taken 15 hours or more. The magic had begun.

I said before that I don't understand the principles of flight. But I do understand that airplanes are strong. Very, VERY strong. So strong in fact that over the years 95.7% of all passengers involved in aircraft crashes have survived. Think of that next time you are worried – 95% survive! If you want to get an idea of how strong an aircraft is, try this. Creep up behind your best friend and stick one finger of each hand in his/her ears. Be careful, as he/she may not still be your best friend at the end of this little experiment. Now try and lift him/her off the floor. Can't do it, huh? Well that's what aircraft wings can do. Those flat, flexible things sticking out at each side of the fuselage are just like very strong fingers. They have air pushing them upwards and together they lift the whole aircraft off the ground. Amazing! So next time you feel a bit of a jolt inflight or look out the window and see the wings bending a little just relax. Those wings are stronger than your fingers!

I want to tell you now about a time I did have a potentially bad experience. But the truth is that without the use of alcohol or strong drugs, it was so well handled that I did not really care. Here's how it happened.

It was a beautiful sunny day and I was lucky enough to be heading on a business trip to New York on Concorde, that most amazing of all flying machines. It was not my first trip on the bird but I was still excited. It was a beautiful sunny day as we took off towards the west. The only way I can describe take-off is that it was a bit like hurtling up stairs in a rocket. Concorde was not quiet, it was not particularly luxurious, but boy was it fast. I had already done an hour in our Heathrow office that morning, we took off at 10:30 and by 10:00 I was expecting to be in the New York office. Bizarre!

We were only a few minutes into the flight when our captain's voice came over the intercom. After the usual pleasantries he told us in that way that only the British can that there was a spot of bother. I forget the exact technical details but I think it was something to do with the rudder. Most of the passengers, myself included, probably did not even realise that Concorde had such a thing. Anyway, nothing to worry about we were reassured, and here was what was going to happen. "I am sorry for the inconvenience but I am afraid we will have to return to Heathrow," came the soothing tones. "That won't take long, and I have already radioed ahead so a replacement Concorde will be waiting for you as soon as we land."

A different planet from 'rail replacement buses!' British Airways had seven Concordes, so luckily they always had a spare one hanging around somewhere, as you do.

"So the only tiny problem," continued the voice of God (or so it seemed), "is that as we have only just taken off we have too much fuel onboard and the plane is too heavy to land." Too heavy to land? Oh no, I thought, is this going to be the old joke about the Englishman the Irishman and the Scotsman arguing about who is going to be thrown off first? Luckily not. "What I am going to do is go out over the Bristol channel, dump most of the fuel, turn around and then fly back to Heathrow."

Dump most of the fuel? Oh no! How much was 'most'? I hoped he had a little gauge like I did on my car with a read out of 'miles remaining'. How many miles was it anyway from Bristol to London? A hundred? I seemed to remember reading somewhere that Concorde averaged 5 gpm. Yes, 5 gallons per mile...so that was an awful lot of petrol he had to dump on the poor fish in the Channel.

The flight back to Heathrow was magical, among the most memorable I have ever taken. The previous day we had actually been visiting friends in Bath so as we returned to London following the line of the M4 motorway flying at about only 10,000 feet I could re-trace the journey I had taken only yesterday. But this time it was like what I imagine it would be like to travel in a rocket-propelled hot air balloon. Oh look down there, that's the service station we didn't stop at! Is that a cow? Are we nearly there yet? Yes, as soon as we turned around we were nearly there, you stupid boy! You are never not 'nearly there' on Concorde.

And so, only 10 minutes later, to the skies above Windsor. "Now," said our captain, "you may not know it, but these poor chaps at Heathrow don't get much chance to practice the old emergency drill stuff. So what I have agreed with them is that they can use our landing this morning for a jolly good practice. So when we land, don't be alarmed, but what you are going to see is these boys and girls racing alongside us in their fire engines and ambulances to see if they still remember the training. OK, now down we go." He didn't quite let out a 'wheeeeeee!' but he might have done.

Relaxed? You bet we were. 99 people all smiling, even though they had just given back their empty champagne glasses. And sure enough as we hit the tarmac with a bit of a bump mind you, it was like the Fisher Price airport out there with all the yellow and red vehicles trundling in parallel trying to keep up with us.

We came to a stop, not at the terminal, but somewhere in the outer reaches of the airfield. Why? Did they really think the plane might explode? (Actually, yes, but the trick is no one bothered to tell us that bit.) So we promptly deplaned and were escorted onto a bus. That was the funniest part. 99 people, 98 of whom had paid thousands of pound to rocket off to New York – I was on an airline 'duty travel' fare - and here they were boarding a bus! Not something to shout about back on the cocktail circuit in St George's Hill.

And so that, dear reader, was my most frightening emergency landing. Thanks to the way it was handled I have not been so scared since the time I dropped a pillow on my foot.

The next day when I was already back in London I saw the newspaper front page headline shrieking "M25 closed as Concorde makes emergency landing!". Too late to be frightened now.

I'd forgotten the details of this flight apart from it was a Monday flight, so I used Google - 25 MAY 1998 Concorde British Airways, G-BOAC While climbing through FL410 a slight rumble was experienced, which turned out to be the separation of a section of the left hand middle elevon (5ft x 3ft). The aircraft returned; large vibration was noted through mach 1.1 with less vibration at mach 0.90 and during final approach.

Copyright Iain Webster

Footnote - Iain Webster with all his experiences still maintains a passion for flying because he was kept safe, no-one was harmed, therefore no attachments were put on it.

DOES WISHFUL THINKING WORK?

Throughout the course of writing this book, I thought about what would make an attractive book cover. I know enough about 'writing' that the cover is apparently very important. It's the reason why you pick a book off a shelf or off the internet. This book means a lot to me too because I have high hopes it will help so many people overcome their fears, get on flights with confidence.....and fly!

I wanted something really special to be a visual metaphor to show you that the 'impossible' can become the 'more than possible'.

I thought a picture of the sky would be compatible with the contents of my book. But, it had to be a real sky, not an illustration in that – your fear is a very real one and should be recognised and respected as such.

The days wore on, and having already spent far too many hours surfing the internet looking for that illusive photo of the sky I still couldn't find that special one. Oh there were thousands of clear skies, blue skies, skies with a bit of cloud, skies with a lot of cloud (nooo!) aircraft wingtips in the sky..........and so on.

Its pertinent now to give you a little bit more background on me. For the most part I am a pragmatist who feels comfortable with facts, evidence, and tangible things. For some strange reason though, I attract 'spiritual people, and for a sceptic that's no mean feat.

Having spent yet another day sitting on my little balcony in the early summer sunshine with my laptop on my knees pouring over the thousands of photos of skies, the desperation to find that 'just right photo' was beginning to frustrate me – hugely! And yes! I did tap on it again which is why my laptop survived and wasn't thrown over the balcony! However, to show you the volume of my despair I used those words one of my 'enlightened friends' had told me of when things get too tough – 'put it out into the Universe/God/Angels'.

I confess, I did! I opened my arms up towards the sky above me and was about to utter some 'come hither Universe/God/Angel words' when – there

– right above me was something I have never seen in my life…………you guessed it – the upside down rainbow.

I grabbed my iphone – it's the only camera I have hence not a perfectly clear photo, but a photo nonetheless, so apologies for quality!

I did struggle to absorb this big beautiful smile in the sky right above me, it really was awesome.

A little more research and I discovered that upside down rainbows are extremely rare, needing almost unique conditions to appear. They are not like normal rainbows which are created with rain drops. Upside rainbows – the proper name is Circumzenthal Arcs – are created by ice crystals, and considering this was a warm early summer's day made this discovery all the more incredible. They are apparently from the 'halo' family which only added to my delight.

So maybe I should add a chapter on 'putting it out to the Universe' for you because I seem to have the evidence of that working. Ha ha ha ha.

I will fly without fear!

Researching, and compiling information to write a comprehensive self-help book on defeating a fear of flying was a personally interesting experience. It reinforced the effectiveness of my 'cure' through NLP and hypno – when, at that perplexing time of my life, I dreaded flights and never thought I'd ever get on a plane again. So please – do try everything you can. Release those fears and become a happy flyer. Good luck – the world is waiting for you.

ACKNOWLEDGEMENTS

Peter McGill for the strapline 'Jettison your Jitters and join the Jetset'; Iain Webster for his witty piece on his Concorde experience; Renee Adcock – Virgin cabin crew; M Edwards – former client; Michael Carroll of the NLP Academy; Jane Lawson for her encouragement and support; Michael Hannan for technical info re function of flying; Kurek Ashley my longtime mentor; Thomas Noack of Plane Spotters; Nicky Hannan for brilliant editing suggestions; Felicity and Aren Griffiths for encouragement in what has been a long process; family and brilliant friends – you know who you are. Thank you all.

LINDA C GILLATT

NLP Master Practitioner, Ericksonian Hypnotherapist, personal counsellor, therapist, multi award winning entrepreneur, corporate trainer, Master of Communication, firewalker.

Author of several literary works, many business articles and subject of feature articles in reputable business magazines and publications.

Owner/Founder of www.welcomecoaching.com

Printed in Great Britain
by Amazon